PRACTICE BOOK

Picture Perfect

Big Dreams

Warm Friends

SIGNATURES

Harcourt Brace & Company
Orlando Atlanta Austin Boston San Francisco Chicago Dallas New York Toronto London

CONTENTS

PICTURE PERFECT

Learning Log / 1-2
What I See / 4-13
Down on the Farm / 14-23
Sometimes / 24-35
Five Little Rabbits / 36-45
I Went Walking / 46-57
Popcorn / 58-68

BIG DREAMS

Big Brown Bear / 2-11
The Chick and the Duckling / 12-23
Cloudy Day, Sunny Day / 24-33
Moving Day / 34-45
Catch Me If You Can! / 46-57
Later, Rover / 58-68

WARM FRIENDS

Hattie and the Fox / 2-11
And I Mean It, Stanley / 12-21
Best of Friends / 22-31
The Shoe Town / 32-43
Making Friends, Keeping Friends / 44-51
Rex and Lilly Playtime / 52-61

Skills and Strategies Index / 62

Cut-Out Fold-Up Books

Yard Sale	7-8
Come In!	17-18
I Can	27-28
What Is in It?	39-40
Walking My Dog	49-50
More Popcorn	61-62
Little Bear and the Painting	5-6
Going for a Ride	15-16
The Sun Is Out	27-28
Little Pig's Room	37-38
Dinosaurs!	49-50
Here Comes Rover	61-62
What the Hen Saw	5-6
Old Things, New Fun	15-16
Your Pet's Best Friend	25-26
If You Had a Mouse	35-36
Friends Always	47-48
Animal Dances	55-56

Copyright © by Harcourt Brace & Company

All rights reserved. No part of this publication may be reproduced or transmitted in any form or by any means, electronic or mechanical, including photocopy, recording, or any information storage and retrieval system, without permission in writing from the publisher.

Permission is hereby granted to individual teachers using the corresponding student's textbook or kit as the major vehicle for regular classroom instruction to photocopy complete pages from this publication in classroom quantities for instructional use and not for resale.

Duplication of this work other than by individual classroom teachers under the conditions specified above requires a license. To order a license to duplicate this work in greater than classroom quantities, contact Customer Service, Harcourt Brace & Company, 6277 Sea Harbor Drive, Orlando, Florida 32887-6777. Telephone: 1-800-225-5425. Fax: 1-800-874-6418 or 407-352-3442.

HARCOURT BRACE and Quill Design is a registered trademark of Harcourt Brace & Company.
Printed in the United States of America

ISBN 0-15-310820-7

4 5 6 7 8 9 10   030   2001 2000 99

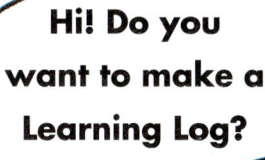   

1. Get some colored paper and some white paper.

2. Staple the paper to make a book.

3. Write *My Learning Log*. Then write your name and draw some pictures on the cover.

Practice Book   YOUR LEARNING LOG   **1**

Down on the Farm

Name _____

> A sentence tells a complete thought.
> **I see a** is not a sentence. **I see a duck** is a sentence.

Look at each picture. Tell a partner about what you see. Use complete sentences when you talk.

PICTURE PERFECT · Practice Book

ORAL LANGUAGE: SENTENCES   19

Name _____

Down on the Farm

A. Say each word. Circle the words that rhyme with *cap*.

cap	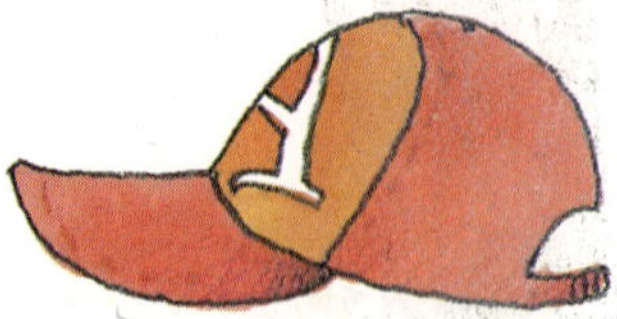
1. (map)	2. top
3. dog	4. (flap)
5. (nap)	6. bat

B. Write another word that rhymes with *cap*. Then draw a picture of it.

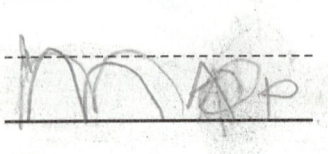

20 WORDS WITH -ap

PICTURE PERFECT Practice Book

Down on the Farm

Name _____

Write the word from the box that best completes each sentence.

| tub   can   on   cab |

1. Duck __can__ see the map.

2. Duck can ride in the __cab__.

3. Duck can play __on__ a mat.

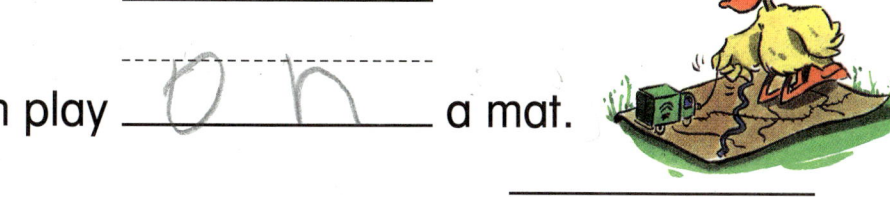

4. Duck can swim in a __tub__.

Think of as many words as you can that end with the letter **b** or the letter **n**. Write the words, or draw pictures of them.

PICTURE PERFECT Practice Book — FINAL CONSONANTS /b/b, /n/n

Name _____

Down on the Farm

Write the word that best completes each sentence.

1. The cat ___plays___ .

   play plays

2. The ___bats___ tap on cans.

   bats bat

3. The hens ___flap___ .
   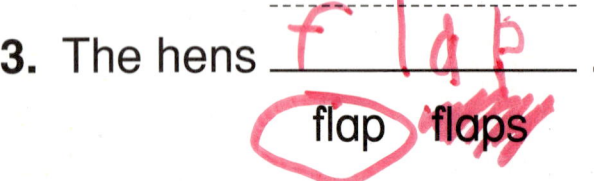
   flap flaps

4. The dog ___yaps___ .

   yap yaps

5. And I ___nap___ !

   naps nap

22 INFLECTIONS: -s

PICTURE PERFECT Practice Book

Sometimes

Name _____

B. Write the word that best completes each sentence.

1. _____ hot.
   I'm   Up
   What can I do?

2. All _____ my friends have a fan.
   on   of
   I do not!

3. _____ of my friends see me.
   All   Am

4. I'm not _____ .
   hen   hot
   I'm happy!

PICTURE PERFECT Practice Book   VOCABULARY   25

Name _____

Sometimes

Think about the story. Draw a picture in each box to complete the story chart.

happy	sad
hot	cold
up	down
red	blue

26 SUMMARIZE AND RETELL

PICTURE PERFECT Practice Book

Sometimes

Name _____

A **sentence** is a group of words. It tells a complete idea. A sentence begins with a capital letter. It ends with a period(.).

Color the machine parts that show sentences. Then write those sentences.

1. _____ .

2. _____ .

3. _____ .

PICTURE PERFECT Practice Book

SENTENCES 29

Name _____

Sometimes

A. Say each word. Circle the words that rhyme with *hot*.

B. Write two other words that rhyme with *hot*.

_____   _____

30 WORDS WITH -*ot*   PICTURE PERFECT Practice Book

Sometimes

Name _____

A. Write a letter from the box to complete each word.

| p | m | d | l | h |

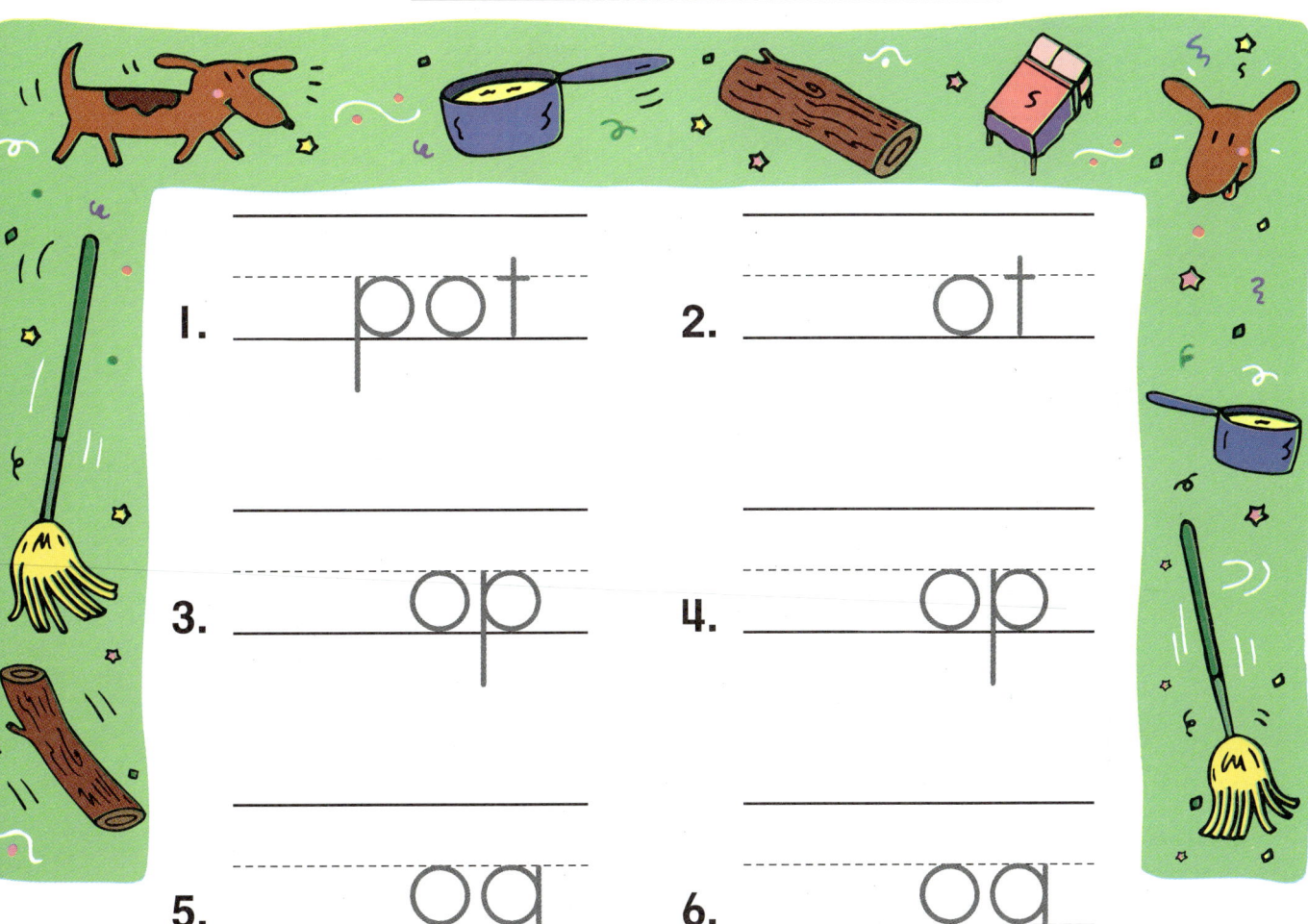

1. ___pot
2. ___ot
3. ___op
4. ___op
5. ___og
6. ___og

B. In these sentences, use two of the words you made.

I have a _____.   Bob likes the _____.

PICTURE PERFECT Practice Book

SHORT VOWEL: /o/o   31

Name _____

Sometimes

Finish each sentence. Write the contraction for the two words below each sentence.

| She's | It's | What's | I'm |

1. _____ a lot like Jan.
   I am

2. _____ my friend.
   She is
   Jan and I like hats.

3. _____ in the blue hat?
   What is

4. _____ my cat! It's Red!
   It is
   Red, Jan, and I all like hats!

Three contractions are the same in one way. What do they all have? One is not the same. What does it have?

Sometimes

Name _____

Make new words. Use the words to finish the sentences.

ca	b	n	p	t
	cab			

_____

1. The _____ is happy.

_____

2. She has a _____ on.

_____

3. She is in the _____ .

_____

4. Her friends _____ go in.

PICTURE PERFECT Practice Book   FINAL CONSONANTS: /b/b, /n/n, /p/p, t/t   35

Name _____

Five Little Rabbits

A. Write the word that tells about the rabbit toy in each box.

| three   little   jumping   big |

a _____ rabbit

a _____ rabbit

a _____ rabbit

_____ rabbits

36 **VOCABULARY** PICTURE PERFECT Practice Book

Five Little Rabbits

Name _____

B. Write the word from the box that completes each sentence.

| One   off   just   he |

1. Will _____ jump?

2. _____ , two, three, GO!

3. He jumped _____ .

4. He _____ did it!

The word OFF has two meanings. Make a list of things someone can jump OFF. Then make a list of things you can turn ON and OFF. Share your lists with a friend.

Name _____

Five Little Rabbits

Think about the story. Draw pictures to show the missing parts of the story.

1.

2.

3.

4.

5.

6.

38 SUMMARIZE AND RETELL

PICTURE PERFECT Practice Book

Five Little Rabbits

Name _____

Words in a sentence are in order. The words must be in order to make sense.

The rabbits' sentences don't make sense. Write the words in order.

on top. I am.

up go. will I

down. come I can

off. You jump can

1. _____ .

2. _____ .

3. _____ .

4. _____ .

PICTURE PERFECT Practice Book | WORD ORDER IN SENTENCES

Name _____

Five Little Rabbits

A. Write four words that rhyme with *fan*.

fan

1. _____

2. _____

3. _____

4. _____

B. Write a word that rhymes with *man* to finish the rhyme. Draw a picture to go with it.

I see a <u>man</u>.

He has a _____ .

42 WORDS WITH -*an*   PICTURE PERFECT Practice Book

Five Little Rabbits

Name _____

Fill in the chart. Then use some of the words to finish the sentences.

	-ed	-ing
play	played	
jump		

1. One rabbit is _____ in a hat.

2. One is _____ up and down.

3. He _____ a lot.

4. Two rabbits _____ on a mat.

PICTURE PERFECT Practice Book

INFLECTIONS: -ed, -ing 43

Name _____

Five Little Rabbits

A. Look at the rabbits. Write *real* or *not real* under each one.

44 REALITY/FANTASY   PICTURE PERFECT Practice Book

Five Little Rabbits

Name _____

**B. Write a word to finish each sentence.
Draw a picture for each sentence.**

REAL

I can _____ a rabbit.

NOT REAL

The rabbit and I will _____ .

PICTURE PERFECT Practice Book   REALITY/FANTASY   **45**

Name _____

I Went Walking

Write the words in the box where they belong.

animals	saw
green	walking
looking	went

red

pink

blue

_____

I see _____ .

I Went Walking

Name _____

_____
- - - - - - - - - - - - - - -
_____

_____
- - - - - - - - - - - - - - -
_____

_____

_____
- - - - - - - - - - - - - - -
I _____ to see my dog.

My dog ran and sat.

_____
- - - - - - - - - - - - - - -
I _____ my dog.

Try This! Writing

What if you woke up and you were green?
What would happen? Write about it.

Name _____

I Went Walking

Think about the story. Draw a line through the maze to show things that happened. Then retell the story to a friend.

48 SUMMARIZE AND RETELL

PICTURE PERFECT Practice Book

I Went Walking

Name _____

> A **telling sentence** tells about something or someone. It begins with a capital letter. It ends with a period (.).

Write these telling sentences correctly.

1. i have a pig

_____
- -
_____

2. he and I play

_____
- -
_____

3. he has a cold nose

_____
- -
_____

4. my pig is my friend

_____
- -
_____

Draw a pet you have or would like to have. Write a telling sentence about it. Use a capital letter and a period.

PICTURE PERFECT Practice Book — TELLING SENTENCES 51

Name _____

I Went Walking

A. Say each word. Circle the words that rhyme with *cat*.

	cat
1. bat	2. cot
3. cap	4. mat
5. pan	6. pat

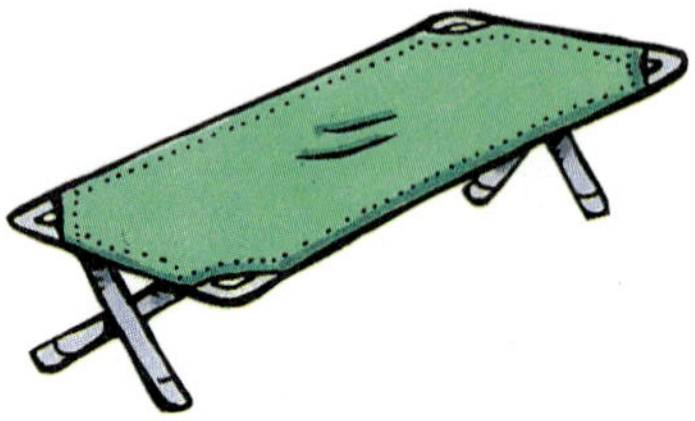

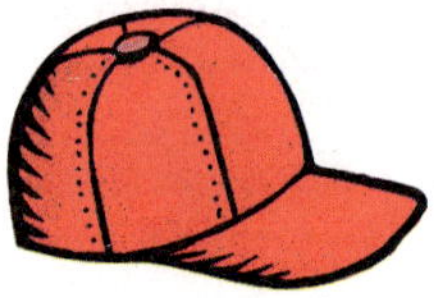

B. Choose two *-at* words. Write an *-at* rhyme. Then draw it.

_____

_____

_____

52 SPELLING *-at*

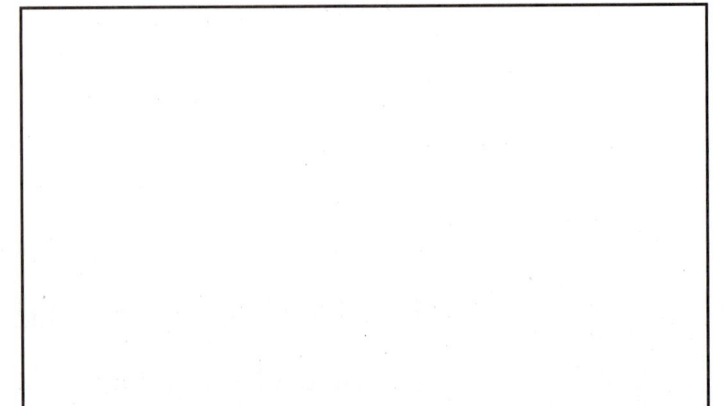

PICTURE PERFECT Practice Book

I Went Walking

Name _____

Write words to make the poem rhyme.

1. I see a bat

   _____

   Up on the _____ .

2. That bat is Hap.

   _____

   He likes to _____ .

3. I see Hap can

   _____

   Fly up on a _____ .

4. My bat can hop

   _____

   Up on a _____ .

Write the alphabet down the side of a sheet of paper.
Write -ap on another sheet. Hold the -ap next to each letter.
How many words can you make?

PICTURE PERFECT Practice Book RHYMING WORDS 53

Name _____

I Went Walking

A. Read each word. Color the space if the animal can fly. Do not color the space if the animal can not fly.

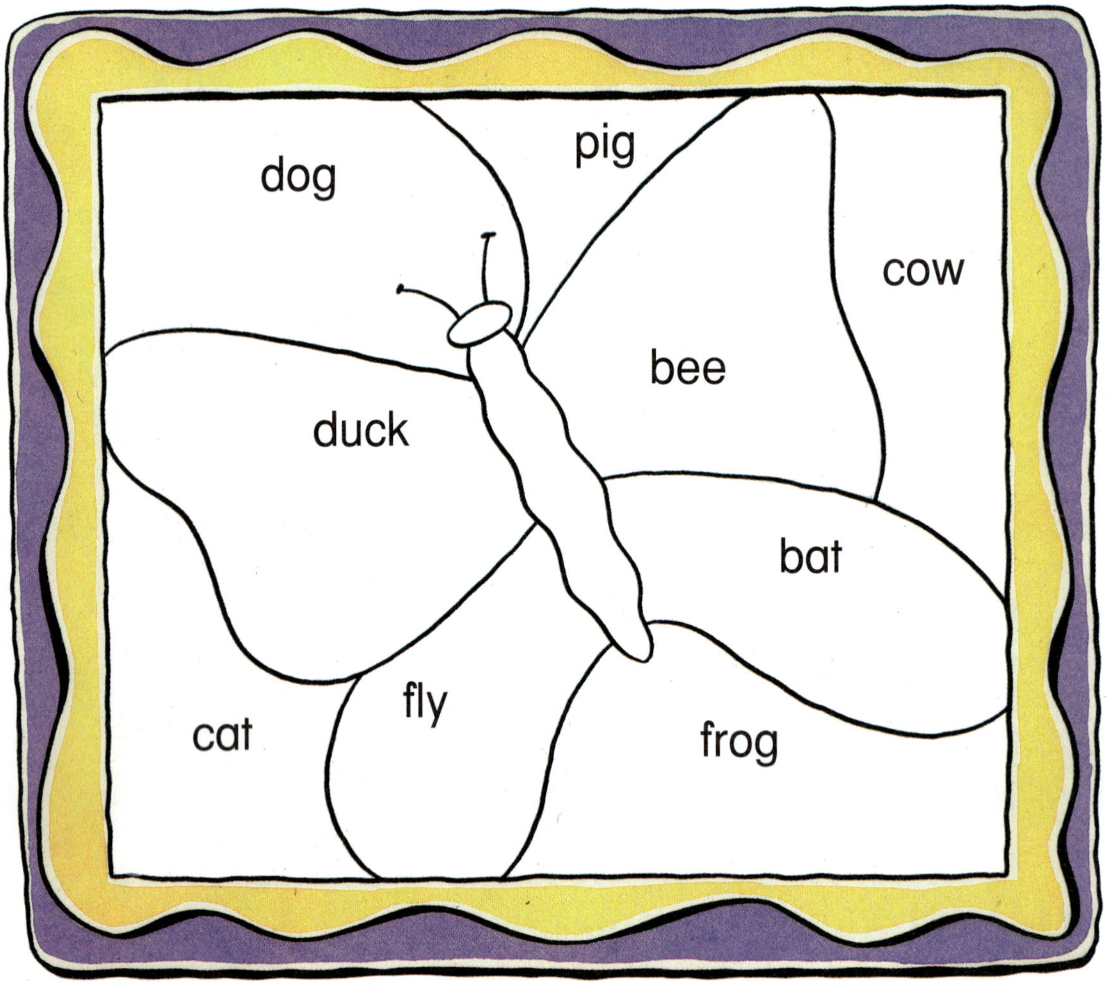

dog pig cow bee duck bat cat fly frog

Can it fly? _____
Write *yes* or *no*.

Make a list of other things that fly.

I Went Walking

Name _____

B. Look at the first animal in each row. Circle the other animals that are like the first one.

SCIENCE

PICTURE PERFECT   Practice Book   CLASSIFYING   55

Name _____

Write the word that best completes each sentence.

1. Pat is _____ the dog.
   walks   walking

2. Pat _____ a lot.
   walks   walking

3. The dog likes _____ .
   played   playing

4. He is _____ up.
   jumping   jumped

5. He _____ off.
   just   jumped

56   INFLECTIONS: -s, -ed, -ing

I Went Walking

Name _____

Write the word that best completes each sentence.

1. I am _____ .

2. I got on top of the _____ .

3. Can you see all the _____ ?

4. The pot is not _____ .

5. I will _____ off the pot.

Draw a big pot. Fill it with words that have a short *o*. Add more of these words as you find them.

PICTURE PERFECT Practice Book   SHORT VOWEL: /o/   57

Name _____

Write the word that best completes each sentence.

1. I _____ the popcorn.
   good   get

2. I _____ it in.
   put   play

3. I do not _____ .
   saw   stop

4. Put in a little _____ .
   me   more

58 VOCABULARY   PICTURE PERFECT Practice Book

Popcorn

Name _____

5. It will come _____ .

    out   one

6. _____ it _____ you can!

   Cat Catch   if I'm

7. _____ like it.

   Will We

8. We _____ happy.

    are am

TRY THIS! Learning Log

Make a list of all the things you can **catch**.
(Don't forget a cold!)

PICTURE PERFECT Practice Book   VOCABULARY   59

Name _____

Popcorn

Think about the story. Draw pictures to show the friends' problem and how they fixed it.

60 SUMMARIZE AND RETELL

PICTURE PERFECT Practice Book

More Popcorn

1

More popcorn!
Put it in the pot.

3

Popcorn—
Up to the top.

6

No more popcorn!
We are going to pop!

8

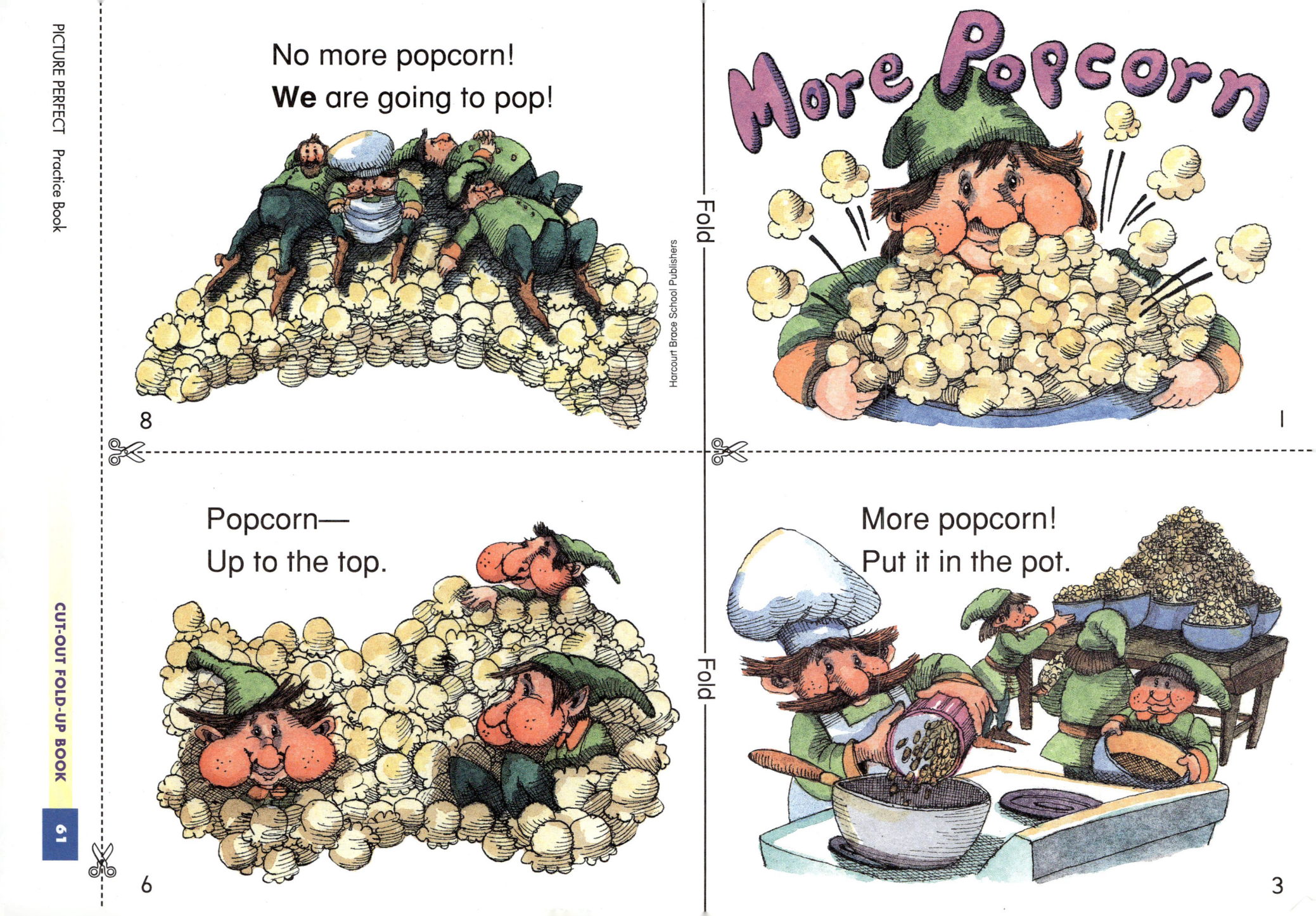

Harcourt Brace School Publishers

PICTURE PERFECT   Practice Book

CUT-OUT FOLD-UP BOOK

61

4

More popcorn!
It's good to have a lot.

2

More popcorn!
It is good and hot.

Harcourt Brace School Publishers

— Fold —   — Fold —

More popcorn!
We like to see it pop.

STOP!

5

7

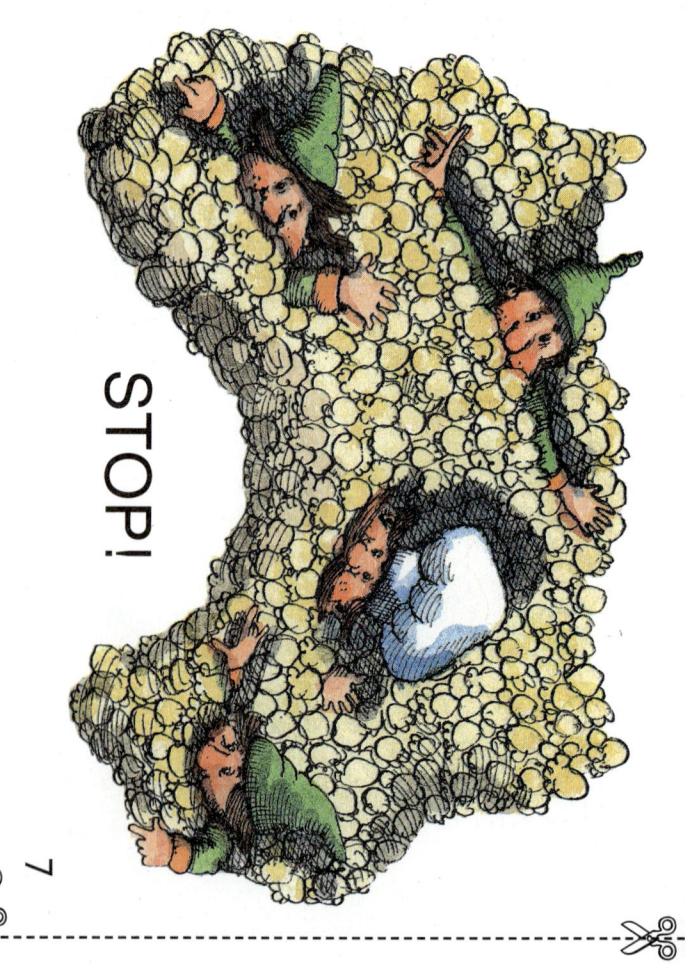

Directions: Help your child cut and fold the book.

62 CUT-OUT FOLD-UP BOOK

PICTURE PERFECT   Practice Book

Popcorn

Name _____

An **asking sentence** asks about something or someone. It begins with a capital letter. It ends with a question mark (?).

Help the cat. Write each asking sentence correctly.

1. _____
2. _____
3. _____
4. _____

is it hot

what can I do

do you like it

will you come get it

PICTURE PERFECT Practice Book

ASKING SENTENCES 63

Name _____

Popcorn

A. Say each word. Circle the words that rhyme with *stop*.

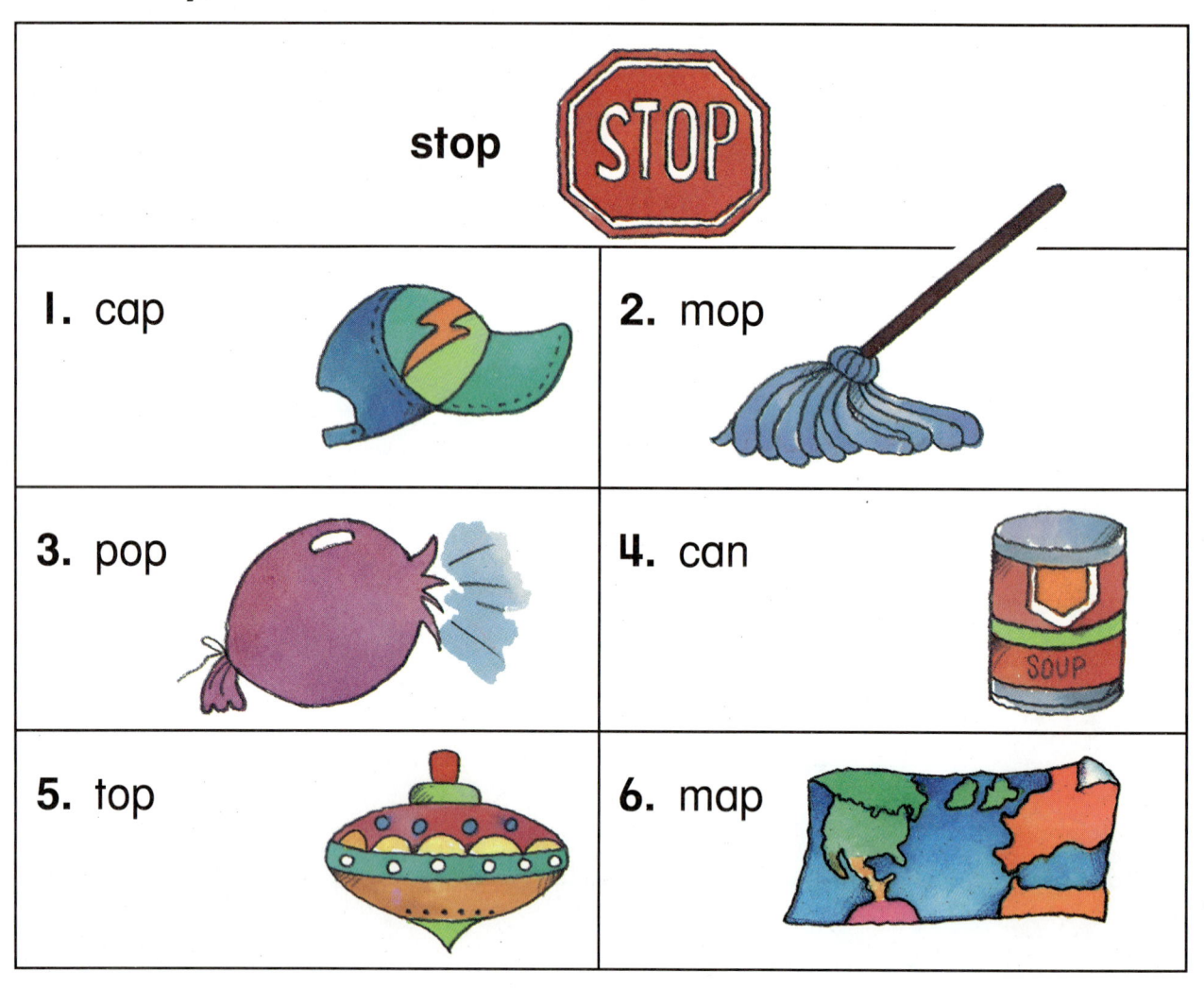

stop	
1. cap	2. mop
3. pop	4. can
5. top	6. map

B. Write another word that rhymes with *stop*. Then draw a picture of it.

_____

64 SPELLING: WORDS WITH -*op*

PICTURE PERFECT Practice Book

Popcorn

Name _____

Use the letters to write three-letter words.

Letters: p, a, f, t, m

1. map
2. ___
3. ___

Letters: p, a, o, t, h

4. ___
5. ___
6. ___

PICTURE PERFECT   Practice Book

LETTER PATTERN: CVC

65

Name _____

Popcorn

Write the word that best completes each sentence.

1. He is _____ .

   Don   got

2. He has a big _____ .

   rob   job

3. He puts things _____ and off.

   on   of

4. It will not get too _____ .

   hot   hop

5. He likes to _____ .

   mob   mop

6. Don has a _____ to do.

   log   lot

66   SHORT VOWEL: /o/

PICTURE PERFECT   Practice Book

Popcorn

Name _____

Look at the picture. Write a word to make a rhyming pair.

fat cat

1. hot _____

2. tan _____

3. flap _____

4. can _____

5. bat _____

6. pop _____

PICTURE PERFECT Practice Book

RHYMING WORDS 67

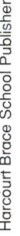

Name _____

Popcorn

Write the word that best completes each sentence.

1. Dog _____ up and down.
   jumps   jumping

2. Cat is _____ up, up, up.
   jump   jumping

3. Hog _____ down.
   walked   walking

4. Fly _____ down.
   look   looked

5. I see ☐ friends _____ .
   jumps   jumping

68   INFLECTIONS: -s, -ed, -ing

PICTURE PERFECT Practice Book

Big Dreams

Name _____

Big Brown Bear

Write the word that best completes each sentence.

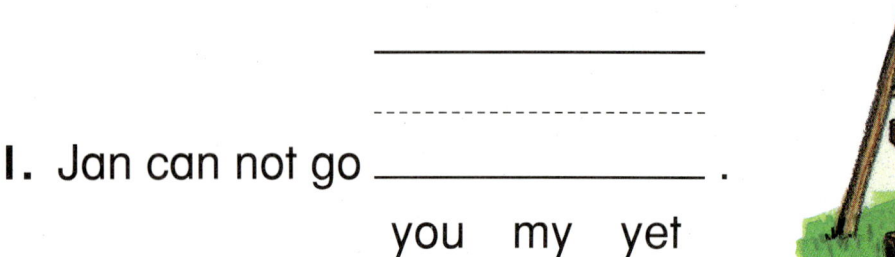

1. Jan can not go _____ .
   you   my   yet

2. Jan gets red and blue _____ .
   play   up   paint

3. Jan is all _____ .
   set   but   saw

4. _____ paints a hen.
   Was   She   Over

5. _____ she paints a cat.
   Yet   Top   Then

2 **VOCABULARY**   BIG DREAMS Practice Book

Big Brown Bear

Name _____

6. Jan _____ blue paint.
   went   has   she

7. _____ she did not see the dog.
   But   Big   Put

8. Jan _____ blue.
   stop   was   he

9. _____ no!
   Do   Oh   Have

10. It was not _____ yet!
    over   of   but

BIG DREAMS   Practice Book

VOCABULARY   3

Name _____

Big Brown Bear

Complete the story frame.

1.  Bear _____

2.  Little Bear _____

3.  Then Bear _____

4.  Little Bear _____

4 SUMMARIZE AND RETELL BIG DREAMS Practice Book

Little Bear and the Painting

1

Then the blue paint ran down.

3

Then the red paint ran down.
Little Bear was sad.

6

It looked just like Little Bear.
Little Bear was happy!

8

Harcourt Brace School Publishers

BIG DREAMS Practice Book

CUT-OUT FOLD-UP BOOK 5

4

Then the green paint ran down.

2

Little Bear was painting.

——Fold—— ——Fold——

Harcourt Brace School Publishers

Then the yellow paint ran down.

5

Then she painted a little brown bear.

7

Directions: Help your child cut and fold the book.

6 CUT-OUT FOLD-UP BOOK

BIG DREAMS Practice Book

Name _____

Complete each rhyme with a word that has the same vowel sound as *pet*.

1. I bet you can see my pet.

    It is up in a ☐☐. (jet)

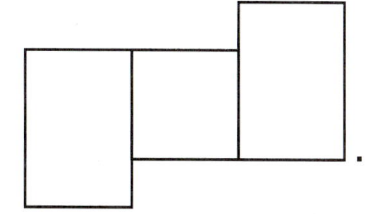

2. Can you see my hen?

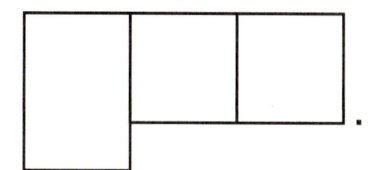

    It is in a ☐☐☐. (pen)

3. Look at little Deb.

    She likes the ☐☐☐. (web)

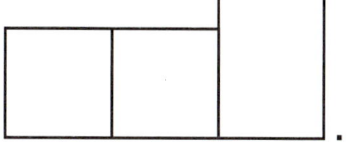

4. My pet is all set.

    It can not get ☐☐☐. (wet)

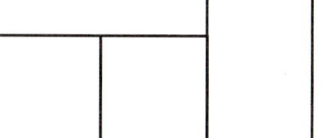

BIG DREAMS Practice Book

SHORT VOWEL: /e/e

9

Name _____

Big Brown Bear

Write the word from the box that best completes each sentence.

ten red yet hen

1. Jen and I like _____ .

2. We have a red _____ .

3. We have _____ red dogs.

4. But we do not have a red jet _____ .

TRY THIS! Learning Log

Make a list of things that are red. Circle all of the words that have the same vowel sound as *red*.

10 SHORT VOWEL: /e/e   BIG DREAMS Practice Book

Big Brown Bear

Name _____

Write the letters that complete each word.

1. _____ an and I went walking.

   Gr   Cr

   We saw a lot.

2. A _____ og was jumping.

   dr   fr

3. A _____ ab was walking.

   pr   cr

   Gran and I got hot.

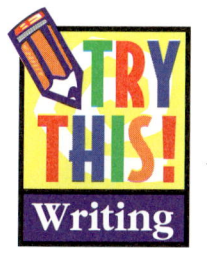

4. Then we saw the _____ ee .

   tr   br

TRY THIS! Writing

Make a word sandwich. Cut out a sheet of paper shaped like a big piece of bread. On it, write words that begin with *br*. Put your bread on a classmate's bread to make a sandwich.

BIG DREAMS Practice Book

INITIAL CLUSTERS WITH *r* 11

Name _____

The Chick and the Duckling

Write the word that best completes each sentence.

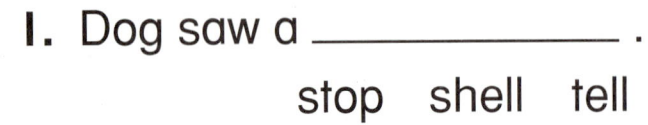

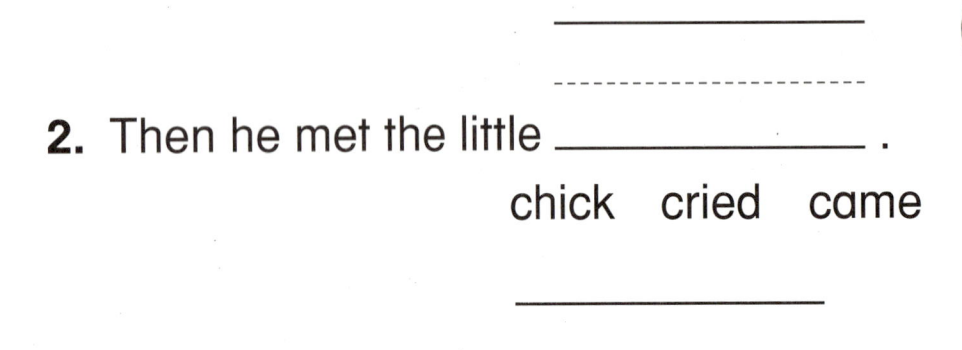

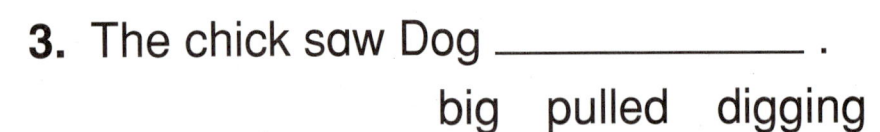

1. Dog saw a _____ .
   stop   shell   tell

2. Then he met the little _____ .
   chick   cried   came

3. The chick saw Dog _____ .
   big   pulled   digging

4. The chick was digging, _____ .
   top   too   went

12 VOCABULARY

BIG DREAMS Practice Book

The Chick and the Duckling

Name _____

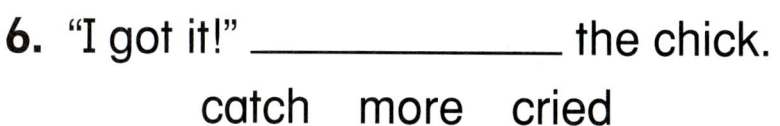

5. Then Dog _____ over.
   came   cat   chick

6. "I got it!" _____ the chick.
   catch   more   cried

7. Dog and the chick _____ it out.
   paint   pulled   shell

8. It was just what Dog was looking _____ .
   too   fly   for

   "Can I have it?" said Dog.

9. "If we can go _____ ," said the chick.
   swimming   saw   telling

   "Yes, we can go swimming," said Dog.

BIG DREAMS Practice Book   VOCABULARY 13

Name _____

The Chick and the Duckling

Think about the story. Put a ✓ next to each thing the character does. Then draw a picture of Duckling doing what Chick does not like to do.

Duckling	Chick
❏ walking	❏ walking
❏ painting	❏ painting
❏ digging	❏ digging
❏ looking for a 🪱	❏ looking for a 🪱
❏ looking for a 🪲	❏ looking for a 🪲
❏ catching a 🦋	❏ catching a 🦋
❏ swimming	❏ swimming
❏ pulling	❏ pulling

14 SUMMARIZE AND RETELL

BIG DREAMS Practice Book

Going for a Ride

1

"Can I have a ride, too?" cried Hen.

3

"Yes, you can," said Duck.

6

Then all of the animals went for a ride!

8

Harcourt Brace School Publishers

BIG DREAMS Practice Book

CUT-OUT FOLD-UP BOOK 15

Duck pulled Chick.

"Yes, you can," said Duck.

"Can I have a ride, too?" cried Rabbit.

Duck pulled Chick, Hen, and Rabbit up to the top.

Directions: Help your child cut and fold the book.

16 CUT-OUT FOLD-UP BOOK

BIG DREAMS Practice Book

The Chick and the Duckling

Name _____

> A sentence has a **naming part.** Sometimes the naming parts of two sentences can be joined.

Use and to join the naming parts of the two sentences. Write the new sentence.

1. The cats ride. The dogs ride.

   _____

   _____

2. The duck will go up. The cow will go up.

   _____

   _____

3. The pig will go. The chick will go.

   _____

   _____

BIG DREAMS Practice Book · JOINING NAMING PARTS · 17

Name _____

The Chick and the Duckling

A. Say each word. Circle the words that rhyme with *shell*.

	shell	
1. fly		2. bell
3. well		4. pot
5. yell		6. hen

B. Use the letters to write three words that rhyme with *shell*.

| e | l | l | f | t | s |

e	l	l

WORDS WITH -ell

BIG DREAMS Practice Book

The Chick and the Duckling

Name _____

Circle the word that names each picture. Write that word on the line.

1. 
_____
sail   sack

2. 
_____
doll   duck

3. 
_____
tell   rock

4. 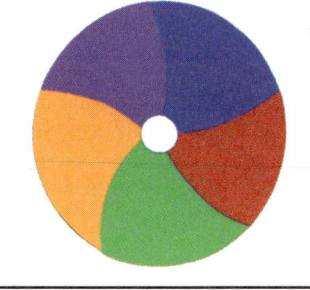
_____
back   ball

5. 
_____
book   bell

6. 
_____
look   well

BIG DREAMS Practice Book

FINAL CONSONANTS: /k/k, ck; /l/l, ll

Name _____

The Chick and the Duckling

Add *ed* and *ing* to make new words. Then use those words to complete the sentences.

	ed						ing				
hop	h	o	p	p	e	d					
nap											
mop											

1. My friends are _____ on the mat.

2. You are _____ just like Pat.

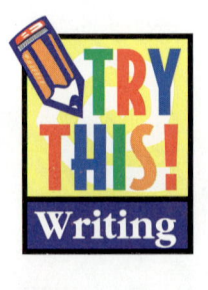

3. I _____ all over.

TRY THIS! Writing

Add *ed* and *ing* to *tap*, *bat*, and *drop*. Don't forget to double the last letter. Use two of your new words in sentences.

20 INFLECTIONS: -ed, -ing   BIG DREAMS Practice Book

The Chick and the Duckling

Name _____

Read each sentence. One word has a line under it. Circle the picture that shows what this word means.

1. The duck walked over the branch.

2. The duck swims in blue water.

3. Ducks do not have shells, but turtles do.

4. Ducks dive down and then come up.

BIG DREAMS Practice Book

CONTEXT CLUES **21**

Name _____

The Chick and the Duckling

5. Three cows have red spots.

6. The cow was catching a fish in the net.

7. At the store, the cow got a hat.

8. The cow rides on a blue tractor.

TRY THIS! Learning Log

When you are reading a sentence and come to a word you don't know, what can you do? Write your answer in your Learning Log.

22   **CONTEXT CLUES**   **BIG DREAMS** Practice Book

The Chick and the Duckling

Name _____

Mix up the letters to make new words. Then use some of your words to complete the sentences.

p n t e	pet		
w b t e			

1. I have a _____ dog.

2. He gets all _____ .

3. I _____ you will like my pet!

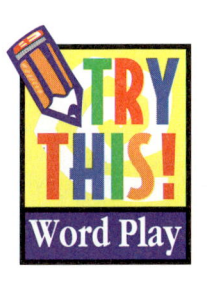

TRY THIS! Word Play

Write these six letters on small paper squares: *l, l, w, s, t, e.* Make some words. Write the words and draw pictures to go with some of them.

BIG DREAMS Practice Book

SHORT VOWEL: /e/e   23

Name _____

Cloudy Day, Sunny Day

Write the words that best complete the letter.

| to sun day fun throw |

Sal,

_____

One _____ you can

_____

come over. If the _____ is out,

we can go swimming. It will be

_____ _____

a day _____ _____ and catch.

_____

We will have lots of _____ !

Jack

24 VOCABULARY

BIG DREAMS Practice Book

Cloudy Day, Sunny Day

Name _____

Write the words that best complete the letter.

| reading   sunny   stay   Let's   running |

Jack,

I was just _____ the map.

One _____ day I will come and I will _____ see you. I will _____ all day. We will go _____ and swimming. _____ go digging for shells, too.

Sal

VOCABULARY 25

Name _____

Cloudy Day, Sunny Day

Complete the chart. Draw a cloud next to each picture of what the characters did when it was cloudy. Draw a sun next to each picture of what the characters did when it was sunny.

26 SUMMARIZE AND RETELL

BIG DREAMS Practice Book

The Sun Is Out

The sun is out.
Let's catch a frog.

The sun is out.
Let's run and play.

The sun was out.
Oh no! LET'S GO!

BIG DREAMS   Practice Book

CUT-OUT FOLD-UP BOOK   27

4

The sun is out.
Let's paint a rock.

2

The sun is out.
Let's walk the dog.

Fold

Fold

Harcourt Brace School Publishers

The sun is out.
Let's jump off the dock.

The sun is out.
Let's have fun all day.

5

7

Directions: Help your child cut and fold the book.

28 CUT-OUT FOLD-UP BOOK

BIG DREAMS Practice Book

Cloudy Day, Sunny Day

Name _____

A sentence has a **telling part.** It tells what someone or something does.

Write the telling part of each sentence.

1. Five friends play.

2. Four friends get wet.

3. Three friends read.

4. Two friends fly.

TRY THIS! Learning Log

Write about things you do with friends on cloudy days and sunny days. Circle the telling parts in your sentences.

BIG DREAMS Practice Book   TELLING PARTS OF SENTENCES   **29**

Name _____

Cloudy Day, Sunny Day

A. Say each word. Circle the words that rhyme with *hen*.

hen

1. pen	2. hop
3. ten	4. kick
5. can	6. men

B. Complete the rhyme. Use words that rhyme with *pen*.

This is Jen.

She is my _____.

Jen walks to Ben.

Jen walks to _____.

30   SPELLING -en

BIG DREAMS   Practice Book

Cloudy Day, Sunny Day

Name _____

Write the word that best completes each sentence.

| balloon | ladder | carrot | happy | Rabbit |

Look up, _____ .

Do you see my _____ ?

I will go up my _____ and get it.

Then I will get you a _____ .

I'm _____ we are friends!

BIG DREAMS Practice Book DOUBLE CONSONANTS **31**

Name _____

Cloudy Day, Sunny Day

Write the contraction for the two words below each sentence. Then write the answer to the riddle.

1. _____ dropping in?
   What is

2. _____ big.
   It is

3. It _____ walk or run.
   did not

4. But it _____ stop.
   can not

5. _____ see what it is. It is hot!
   Let us

It's the _____ .

It's

Let's

didn't

can't

What's

32 CONTRACTIONS: n't, 's

BIG DREAMS Practice Book

Cloudy Day, Sunny Day

Name _____

Write *r* as the second letter in each word to make new words. Then use some of the new words to complete the sentences.

fog	+r	frog
tap	+r	
cab	+r	
tack	+r	

1. A _____ and a _____ are friends.

2. The friends go down the _____ .

Will the frog and the crab come back?

TRY THIS! Writing

Write about the trip. Tell if the frog and the crab come back home.

BIG DREAMS Practice Book

INITIAL CLUSTERS WITH *r* 33

Name _____

Moving Day

Write the word that best completes each sentence.

1. _____ is a big job.
   The   This   Then

2. Can you get the little _____?
   box   big   but

3. _____ up the little box.
   Pie   Chick   Pick

4. _____ get the big one.
   I'll   It   It's

5. My shells _____ in it.
   what   were   will

34 VOCABULARY

BIG DREAMS Practice Book

Moving Day

Name _____

6. I had lots of things in this _____ .
                                         are   running   room

7. We will miss _____ pals.
                 one   old   not

8. We will _____ friends.
            make   more   me

9. It is _____ to go.
        two   this   time

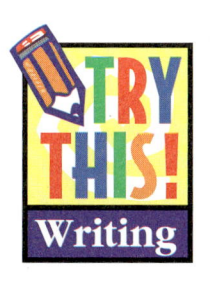

TRY THIS! Writing

Make a list of all the things you can think of that are old. Share your list with a friend.

BIG DREAMS Practice Book   VOCABULARY   35

Name _____

Moving Day

Think about the story and write what happened.

In the beginning

In the middle

At the end

36 SUMMARIZE AND RETELL

BIG DREAMS Practice Book

Little Pig's Room

1

"Can you pick up this room?"
"Yes," said Little Pig. "I can."

3

"Yes," said Little Pig.
"I can." And he did.

8

Harcourt Brace School Publishers

"What is it, Little Pig?"
"I like my old room," Little Pig said.

6

BIG DREAMS   Practice Book

CUT-OUT FOLD-UP BOOK   37

2

"Can you make this bed?" Dad said.
"Yes," said Little Pig. "I can."

4

"Can you fill up this box?" said Little Pig. "I can."
"Yes," said Little Pig. "I can."

7

"Oh," Dad said. "OK."
"Can you tip over this box?"

5

"This is more like it!" Dad said.

Directions: Help your child cut and fold the book.

38 CUT-OUT FOLD-UP BOOK

BIG DREAMS Practice Book

Moving Day

Name _____

A sentence has a **telling part.** Sometimes the telling parts of two sentences can be joined.

Use the word <u>and</u> to join the telling parts. Write the new sentences.

1. Fly packs. Fly flaps.
   _____
   _____

2. Fly looks. Fly dips.
   _____
   _____

3. Fly stops. Fly walks in.
   _____
   _____

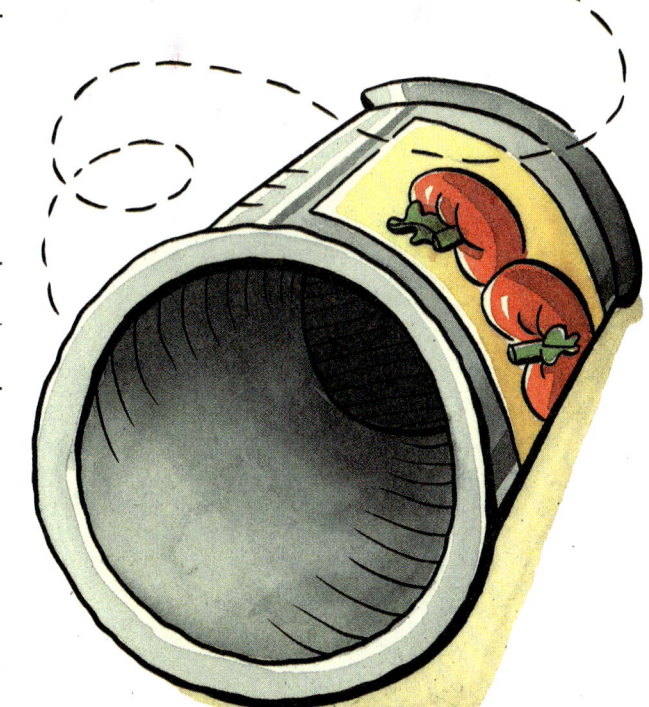

Name _____

Moving Day

A. Say each word. Circle the words that rhyme with *chick*.

chick

1. stick	2. string
3. broom	4. brick
5. kick	6. king

B. Write another word that rhymes with *chick*. Then draw a picture to go with your word.

_____

WORDS WITH -*ick*

BIG DREAMS Practice Book

Moving Day

Name _____

Cut out the cards. Match words and pictures. See if you are right. Turn the cards over. Do they match?

bib	pin	pig
lips	fin	rip

BIG DREAMS Practice Book

SHORT VOWEL: /i/i (CVC) 41

Name _____

Moving Day

42 **SHORT VOWEL:** /i/ *i* **(CVC)**

BIG DREAMS Practice Book

Moving Day

Name _____

Finish the puzzles. Write the letter that makes each word match its picture clue.

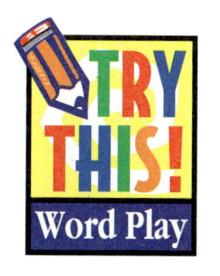

m   d   x

1. f
    o
    s i ☐

2. h
    a
    m o ☐

3. b
    e
    s a ☐

4. l
    i
    r e ☐

TRY THIS! Word Play

See how many words you can write that rhyme with *sad*. Can you make a poem?

BIG DREAMS Practice Book   FINAL CONSONANTS: /ks/x, /m/m, /d/d   43

Name _____

Moving Day

Read the sentences. Write the words from the van that mean the same as the words with lines under them. Then answer the riddle.

Let us   can not
He is   is not
It is

1. <u>It's</u> big and blue.

2. It <u>isn't</u> a box.

3. You <u>can't</u> pick it up.

4. <u>He's</u> going to ride in it.

5. <u>Let's</u> see what it is.

What is it?
Draw your answer.

44   CONTRACTIONS: n't, 's

BIG DREAMS   Practice Book

Moving Day

Name _____

Write the word that best completes each sentence.

1. A fly is on my nose. _____ at it!
   Look   Cook   Like

2. Oh! It bit my _____!
   pick   back   bell

3. It _____ not get me.
   tell   win   will

4. I'm going to _____ up and go.
   back   pack   pal

5. See you, _____!
   pal   pill   pull

6. Do not _____ the fly that I am going!
   look   tell   tick

BIG DREAMS Practice Book   FINAL CONSONANTS: /l/l, ll; /k/k, ck   **45**

Name _____

Catch Me If You Can!

Write the word that best completes each sentence.

1. Is _____ pet big?
   you   yet   your

2. My pet is _____ big.
   happy   when   very

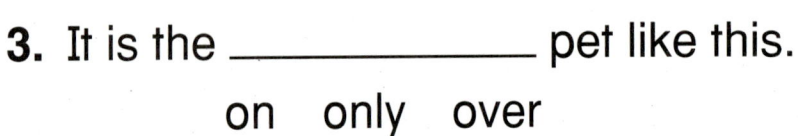

3. It is the _____ pet like this.
   on   only   over

4. We are not big like _____.
   them   the   three

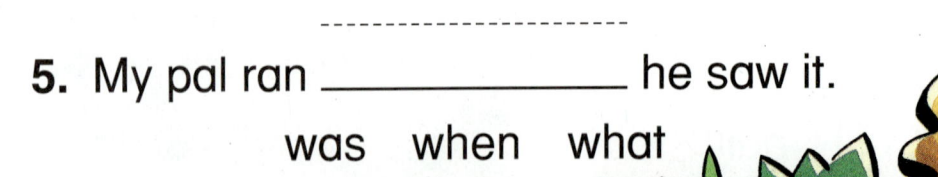

5. My pal ran _____ he saw it.
   was   when   what

46 VOCABULARY

BIG DREAMS Practice Book

Catch Me If You Can!

Name _____

6. He hid _____.
   cried   quickly   can

7. _____ mom ran to see my pet.
   Hen   His   He

8. My pet will walk _____.
   by   but   bee

9. I _____ my pet dinosaur!
   little   let's   love

10. I love it very _____.
   my   much   mop

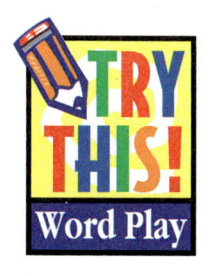

TRY THIS! Word Play

Draw the best pet you can imagine.
Write three words to describe it.

BIG DREAMS   Practice Book

VOCABULARY   47

Name _____

Catch Me If You Can!

Think about the story. Look at the pictures and write what happened next.

They saw how big he was.

THEN
_____
_____
_____

She said, "Catch me if you can!"

THEN
_____
_____
_____

He got her!

THEN
_____
_____
_____

Dinosaurs!

1

All dinosaurs came out of eggs. Look at them!

3

But kids love dinosaurs—very, very much!

Harcourt Brace School Publishers

8

This dinosaur had big teeth!

6

BIG DREAMS   Practice Book

CUT-OUT FOLD-UP BOOK   49

4

This dinosaur ran quickly.

2

Dinosaurs were big—very, very big!

Harcourt Brace School Publishers

—Fold—

—Fold—

This dinosaur fed only on green things.

5

We have only the bones of dinosaurs.

7

Directions: Help your child cut and fold the book.

50 CUT-OUT FOLD-UP BOOK

BIG DREAMS Practice Book

Catch Me If You Can!

Name _____

A **sentence** tells one whole thought. It has a naming part and a telling part. It begins with a capital letter. It may end with a period (.). It may end with a question mark (?).

Which dinosaurs are saying sentences? Circle three sentences. Then write them.

- We are big.
- Do you like me?
- jumping a lot
- a bee
- I love you.

1. _____

2. _____

3. _____

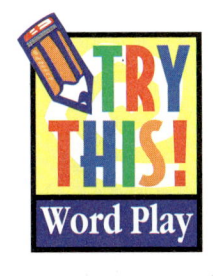

TRY THIS! Word Play

Draw a funny dinosaur. Write what it might be saying.

BIG DREAMS Practice Book · IS IT A SENTENCE? · 51

Name _____

Catch Me If You Can!

A. Say each word. Circle the words that rhyme with *flip*.

flip

1. cap	2. ship
3. wheel	4. drip
5. lip	6. mop

B. Write another word that rhymes with *flip*. Then draw a picture to go with your word.

52 WORDS WITH -*ip*

BIG DREAMS Practice Book

Catch Me If You Can!

Name _____

Look at the picture and the words in the quilt. Write each word in the speech balloon where it belongs.

_____!

It's the _____!

_____ it!

_____!

Quick
Quit
queen
Quack

DIGRAPH: /kw/ qu

Name _____

Catch Me If You Can!

A. The pictures are out of order. Write the number 1, 2, or 3 by each one to show which happened first, second, and last. Then write the sentences in order so they tell a story.

___   ___   ___
Mom got mad.   Dan went in.   Dan jumped.

1. _____

2. _____

3. _____

54 SEQUENCE

Catch Me If You Can!

Name _____

B. Dino wants to leave Camp Wannagohome. But his letter is out of order. Write it again. Put it in order.

Mom and Dad,

_____
- -
_____
_____
_____
_____
_____
- -
_____

Come and get me!
Love,
Dino

We go to bed at 8. No TV!
We have green things to eat at 7.
They get me up at 6.
Then we have to swim all day.

TRY THIS! Math

Draw a clock. Tell what you do at the time on the clock.

Name _____

Catch Me If You Can!

Write the contraction for the two words below each sentence. Then make up a good answer to the riddle.

can't   It's   don't   Isn't   What's

1. _____ in the box?
   What is

2. I _____ see a thing.
   do not

3. It _____ fly.
   can not

4. _____ it fun to play with?
   Is not

5. _____ got a cold nose.
   It has

It is a _____ !

56 CONTRACTIONS: n't, 's   BIG DREAMS Practice Book

Catch Me If You Can!

Name _____

Write each word from the box under the picture with the same ending sound.

fix	dad	six	ham	ax
mom	hid	red	him	

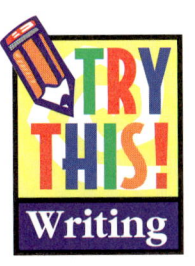

box   bed   jam

_____   _____   _____
_____   _____   _____
_____   _____   _____
_____   _____   _____

TRY THIS! Writing

Choose two of the words from the box and use them in one sentence.

FINAL CONSONANTS: /ks/x, /d/d, /m/m

Name _____

Later, Rover

Write the word that best completes each sentence.

1. Mop _____ to play.
   went   were   wants

2. "_____, Mop," said Dick.
   Hello   Have   He

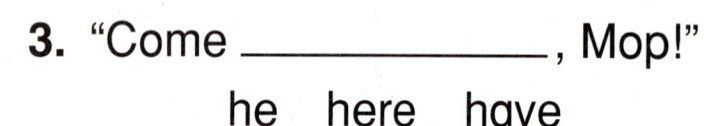

3. "Come _____, Mop!"
   he   here   have

4. "You can play _____ me."
   with   where   was

5. Mop ran over _____.
   the   three   there

58 VOCABULARY

BIG DREAMS Practice Book

Later, Rover

Name _____

6. Mop jumped over and over _____.
                am   again   away

7. He liked that _____.
          game   get   same

8. "Stop _____," said Dick.
      now   no   new

9. "It is time for me to _____."
          at   ever   eat

10. Then Mop played by _____.
          hello   himself   he

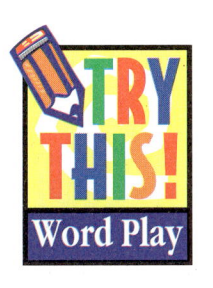

TRY THIS! Word Play

How many good names for dogs can you think of? Make a list.

Name _____

Later, Rover

Think about the story. The people below all said "Later." Circle the picture of the person they said "Later" to. Write why they said it.

1.  Mom said "Later" to ⬚ .

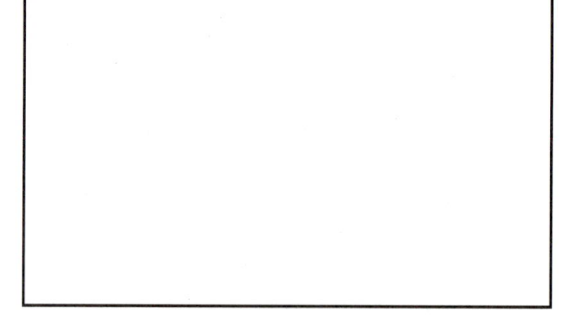

2.  Dad said "Later" to ⬚ .

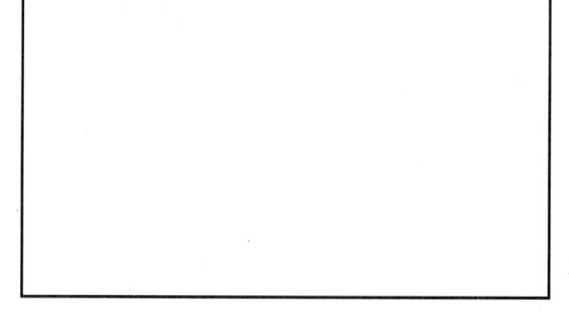

3.  Amy said "Later" to ⬚ .

4.  Andy said "Later" to ⬚ .

SUMMARIZE AND RETELL

BIG DREAMS Practice Book

Here Comes Rover

1

Jill wants to jump with Dick, but here comes Rover.

3

Now Jill wants to eat pie.

6

Good dog, Rover! Good dog!

8

BIG DREAMS Practice Book
CUT-OUT FOLD-UP BOOK 61

2

Jill wants to play a game,
but here comes Rover.

4

Jill wants to throw a ball,
but here comes Rover.

Here comes Rover.
Oh, no! Not again!

Jill wants to catch a butterfly,
but here comes Rover.

5

7

Directions: Help your child cut and fold the book.

62 CUT-OUT FOLD-UP BOOK

BIG DREAMS Practice Book

Later, Rover

Name _____

> The word *I* is always written as a capital letter.
> A telling sentence ends with a **period** (.).
> An asking sentence ends with a **question mark** (?).

Write each sentence correctly.

1. i am little
2. i like to play
3. i am up here
4. what am i

1. _____

2. _____

3. _____

4. _____

Name _____

Later, Rover

A. Say each word. Circle the words that rhyme with *dad*.

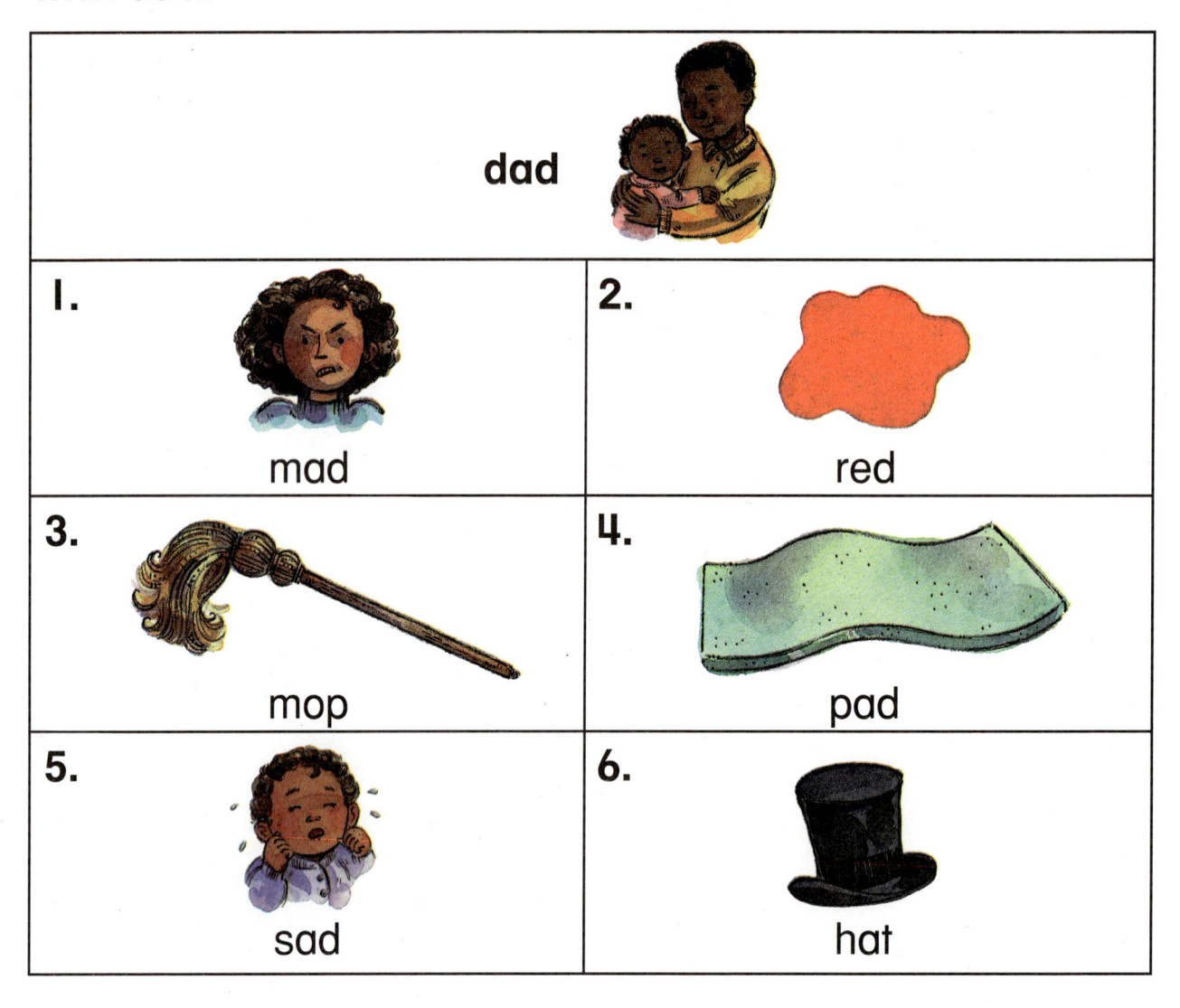

dad	
1. mad	2. red
3. mop	4. pad
5. sad	6. hat

B. Make up a rhyme. Use some of these words:
sad, had, bad, Dad, mad.

_____
_____
_____
_____
_____

64 WORDS WITH *-ad* BIG DREAMS Practice Book

Later, Rover

Name _____

Look at the word parts. Put them together to make a new word. Circle the picture that matches the new word.

1. in   to
   _____

2. bed   room
   _____

3. out   doors
   _____

4. see   saw
   _____

5. mit   ten
   _____

TRY THIS! Word Play

Make up your own new word out of two words you know. Draw a picture to show what it means.

BIG DREAMS Practice Book   WORD PARTS   **65**

Name _____

Later, Rover

Read the sentences. Then write the character and setting for each story.

1. The hen was in the pig pen. She liked to dig. She wanted to be a pig with a fat, pink nose. All the animals looked at her.

Character	Setting

2. Fred the Frog will not come out of his room. He has a cold. He has a red nose. His friends can not see him.

Character	Setting

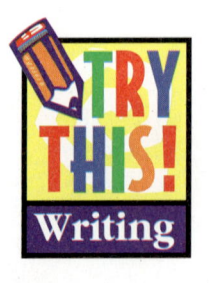

TRY THIS! Writing

Pretend you are writing a story. The setting is the zoo. Write a list of characters you might find there.

66 STORY ELEMENTS

Later, Rover

Name _____

Say each word in the box. Then choose four words to draw about. Draw things a kid can do. Write the word that tells about each thing.

Things a Kid Can Do

sit   dig   grin   lick   swim   sip   win

1.

2.

3.

4.

BIG DREAMS   Practice Book

SHORT VOWEL: /i/i   67

Name _____

Later, Rover

Write the word that best completes each sentence.

| Then went Get yelled hello |

1. I said _____ to a big animal.

2. _____ I was on top!

3. The big animal _____ running.

4. "Stop!" I _____ .

5. "_____ me off now!"

He did!

SHORT VOWEL: /e/e

Warm Friends

Name _____

Hattie and the Fox

Write the words that complete the poem.

body
that
long
dear

Said the dog to the cat,

"Will you just look at _____!"

_____

"Oh, _____ me, what is it?"

said the dog.

_____

"It is _____, and it's big.

It's a bit like a pig,

_____

with a _____ that looks

like a log."

2   VOCABULARY   WARM FRIENDS Practice Book

Hattie and the Fox

Name _____

| None |
| flew |
| away |
| So |
| next |
| Anything |

"_____ I can do?"

said the hen. Then she _____.

_____ the big dog

went running _____.

Cat did not yell hello.

She just got up to go.

_____ of them went

back there the _____ day.

Name _____

Hattie and the Fox

Think about the story. Look at the pictures. Circle YES if the picture shows something that happened in the story. Circle NO if it shows something that did not happen.

YES NO	YES NO
YES NO	YES NO
YES NO	YES NO

Now write what you liked best in the story.

_____
_____
_____
_____

SUMMARIZE AND RETELL — WARM FRIENDS Practice Book

What the Hen Saw

"So what!" said the dog.

"With a long, long body.
Can you see it, too?"

Away the dog ran.
And away the hen flew.

Harcourt Brace School Publishers

4

"It's a very big cat."

2

Hen said, "I see a cat."

— Fold —

Harcourt Brace School Publishers

— Fold —

"So what!" said the dog.

5

"Yes, I do," said the dog.
"So long!" he said.

7

Directions: Help your child cut and fold the book.

6 CUT-OUT FOLD-UP BOOK

WARM FRIENDS Practice Book

Hattie and the Fox

Name _____

Some words are **naming words.** Many naming words name **people.**

Write the best naming word next to each picture. Draw another person in the last box. Write a word that names the person.

friends   gram   mom   vet   dad

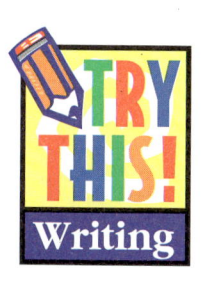

TRY THIS! Writing

Draw a picture of yourself. Write three naming words you could use to tell about yourself.

WARM FRIENDS   Practice Book

NAMING WORDS FOR PEOPLE   7

Name _____

Hattie and the Fox

A. Say each word. Circle the words that rhyme with *chin*.

chin →

1. pan
2. fin
3. bin
4. cap
5. pin
6. bun

B. Draw lines between *in* and the words that rhyme with it. Write the words.

tin   tan   rim   win

in

8   WORDS WITH -*in*   WARM FRIENDS Practice Book

Hattie and the Fox

Name _____

Read the clue. Write the letter that completes the word.

1. a big chick ___ en

2. went quickly ___ an

3. make a little jump ___ op

4. animal friends ___ ets

5. what you play ___ ame

6. what you like to have ___ un

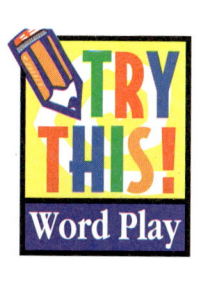

TRY THIS! Word Play

Think of a word. Write a clue. Take off the first letter. Ask a friend to guess your word.

Name _____

Hattie and the Fox

A. Write 1, 2, and 3 to put the pictures in order. Then write what happened first, second, and third.

Hen ran away.

Fox wanted to catch Hen.

Then Hen flew up.

1. _____

2. _____

3. _____

10 SEQUENCE

WARM FRIENDS Practice Book

Hattie and the Fox

Name _____

B. Now write 1, 2, and 3 to put the rest of the story pictures in order. Read the sentences on both pages to tell the story.

| Then Hen flew down. | The wet fox ran away. | Fox did not stop. |

1. _____

2. _____

3. _____

TRY THIS! Writing

Write three sentences about things you do every day. Write them in order.

WARM FRIENDS Practice Book   SEQUENCE   11

Name _____

And I Mean It, Stanley

Write the word that best completes each sentence.

_____

1. I like _____ friends.
   making   when   mom

_____

2. Do you _____ get mad at your friend?
   over   eat   ever

_____

3. I _____ I do.
   know   now   throw

_____

4. Not one _____ is fun when you are mad.
   thing   this   them

_____

5. It's no fun playing by _____ .
   making   myself   away

12 VOCABULARY

WARM FRIENDS Practice Book

And I Mean It, Stanley

Name _____

6. My friend and I _____ to make up.
      see   need   net

7. So I go to _____ to my friend.
      time   talk   top

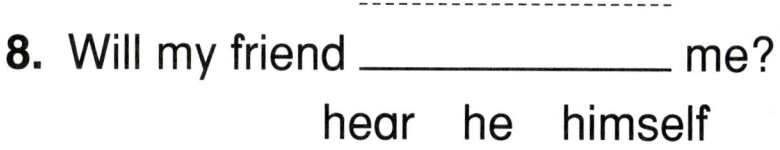

8. Will my friend _____ me?
      hear   he   himself

9. Yes! My friend is not _____ a little mad now.
      one   when   even

10. We are _____ friends again.
      best   long   away

TRY THIS! Learning Log

In your Learning Log, write some things you can say to make up with a friend.

Name _____

And I Mean It, Stanley

Complete the story frame.

Beginning

Middle

Ending

Old Things, New Fun

by _____

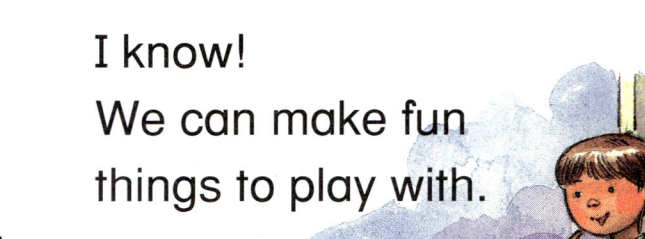

I know!
We can make fun things to play with.

What do you want to make? Draw it.

I can hear you, too.

4

I need a tin can.
You need one, too.

---Fold---

2

What a bad day!
What can we do?

---Fold---

Harcourt Brace School Publishers

I will talk now.
I can hear myself.

5

Let's stay here.
This is the best time we ever had.

7

Directions: Help your child cut and fold the book.

16   CUT-OUT FOLD-UP BOOK

WARM FRIENDS   Practice Book

And I Mean It, Stanley

Name _____

Some naming words name **places**, **animals**, or **things**.

Write each word in the correct web.

cow   dog   paint   game   room   box   hill   chick

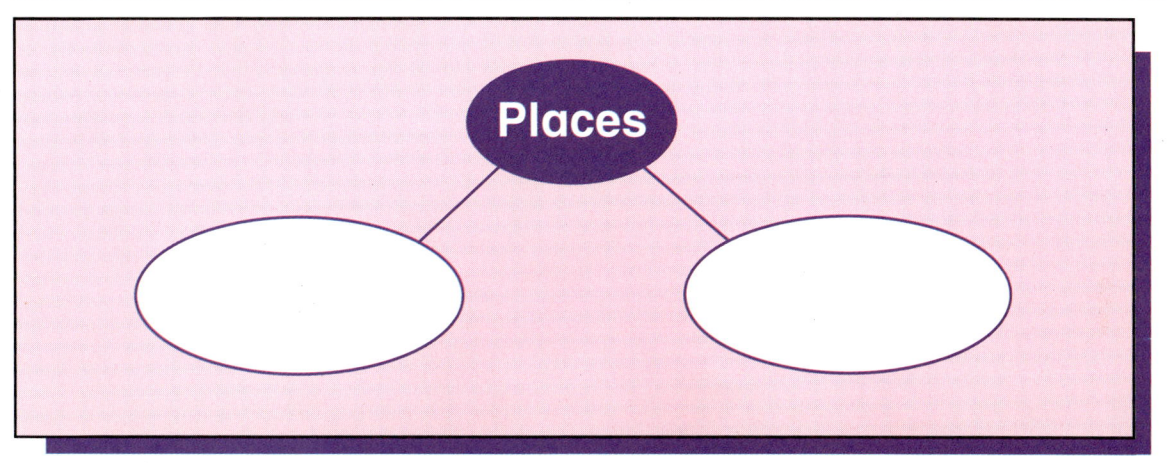

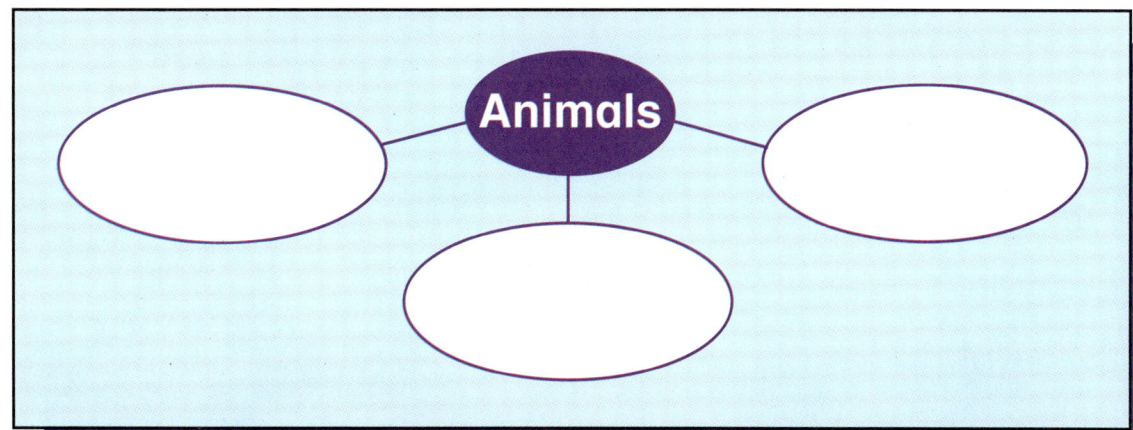

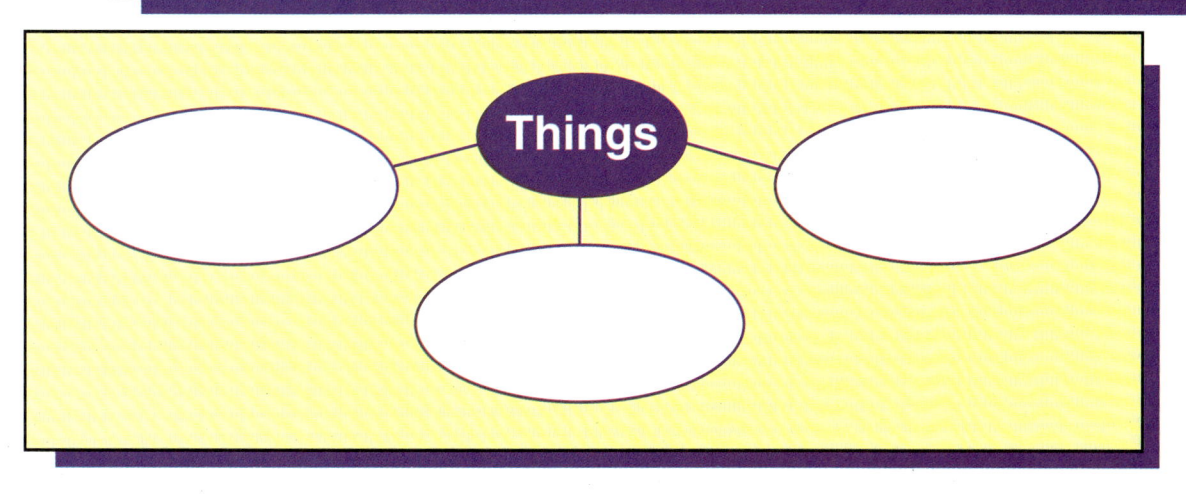

Places

Animals

Things

WARM FRIENDS Practice Book — NAMING WORDS FOR PLACES, ANIMALS, AND THINGS — 17

Name _____

And I Mean It, Stanley

A. Complete each sentence with a word that rhymes with *drill*. Write the word in the puzzle.

	¹m	i	l	l
²				
³				
⁴				

1. Little Red Hen went to the ___.
2. Did you ___ up the box?
3. Jill went up the ___.
4. Bill ___ play a game with you.

B. Use words that end with *-ill* to complete the sentence.

_____ can make hot dogs on the _____.

18 SPELLING *-ill*

WARM FRIENDS Practice Book

And I Mean It, Stanley

Name _____

Write the word that best completes each sentence.

1. Patch is my pup.

   She is _____ a friend to me!

   such   sun

2. Patch and I play _____ .

   cot   catch

3. She licks me on the _____ . No, Patch!

   inch   chin

4. Patch gets a _____ .

   bath   bat

5. _____ she has a long nap.

   Three   Then

WARM FRIENDS Practice Book

DIGRAPHS /ch/ch, tch; /th/th

19

Name _____

And I Mean It, Stanley

Read the clue. Write the words that best complete each sentence. Tell how you know.

| a chick   a friend   a box   an animal |

1. A cat is one.
   A dog is one, too.
   So is a bat.

   It is _____ .

   I know that _____
   _____
   _____

2. It came out of a shell.
   It can fly.
   It is a little hen.

   It is _____ .

   _____
   I know that _____
   _____

20 DRAWING CONCLUSIONS   WARM FRIENDS Practice Book

And I Mean It, Stanley

Name _____

3. You play games with him.
You go swimming with him.
You like him the best.
_____
- -
He is _____ .

_____
- -
I know that _____
_____
- -
_____

4. You can put things in it.
You can get into a big one.
It can have a top. 
_____
- -
It is _____ .

_____
- -
I know that _____
_____
- -
_____

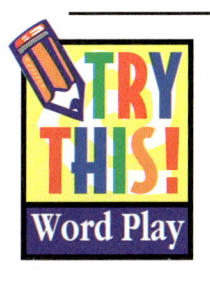

TRY THIS! Word Play

Make up a funny riddle. Let a friend try to answer it.

WARM FRIENDS Practice Book

DRAWING CONCLUSIONS **21**

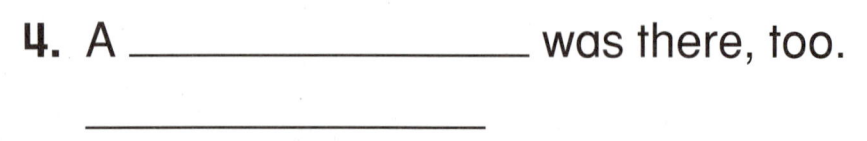

Name _____

Best of Friends

Write the word that best completes each sentence.

boy   Uncle   party   girl   always

1. I went to a _____ with my friend Sam.

2. I _____ like a party.

3. A _____ was there.

4. A _____ was there, too.

5. _____ Sam came to eat.

22 VOCABULARY

WARM FRIENDS Practice Book

Best of Friends

Name _____

same   bugs   her   name   muddy

6. My friend and _____ Uncle Sam have fun.

7. Her _____ is Sam. His name is Sam.

8. They have the _____ name.

9. The party was wet. Then it was _____.

10. The _____ came out.

It was time to go!

TRY THIS! Activity

Draw a picture of your best friend.
Write a sentence that tells why you like your friend.

WARM FRIENDS Practice Book   VOCABULARY 23

Name _____

Best of Friends

Think about the story. Put a ✓ next to the things the boy does and his friends do.

- ❏ look at bugs
- ❏ look for shells
- ❏ go to a 🎉
- ❏ ride 🚲🚲
- ❏ dig a 🌱
- ❏ swim

- ❏ play with a pet 🐸
- ❏ jump on the bed
- ❏ eat 🍪
- ❏ ride a 🐴
- ❏ play ⚾
- ❏ paint

Who is the boy's real best friend? Tell why you think so.

_____
_____
_____
_____

24 SUMMARIZE AND RETELL

WARM FRIENDS Practice Book

Your Pet's Best Friend

1

Your pet likes to do what you do.
You can look the same just for fun.

3

Yes, your pet likes the same things you do. She loves you!

8

Harcourt Brace School Publishers

You can always have fun playing games.

6

4

When it's not muddy,

2

Your pet is your very best friend.
Are you her best friend, too?

---Fold--- ✂ ---Fold---

Harcourt Brace School Publishers

go for a long walk with your pet.

"Get it, girl!"

5

7

Directions: Help your child cut and fold the book.

26 CUT-OUT FOLD-UP BOOK

WARM FRIENDS Practice Book

Best of Friends

Name _____

> The **special name** of a person begins with a capital letter.
> The **special title** of a person begins with a capital letter.

Read the sentences. Write the special names and special titles.

1. We always have fun with uncle rick.

2. One day he went swimming with jan and me.

3. My friend pat brown cut himself on a shell.

4. We went with him to see dr. day.

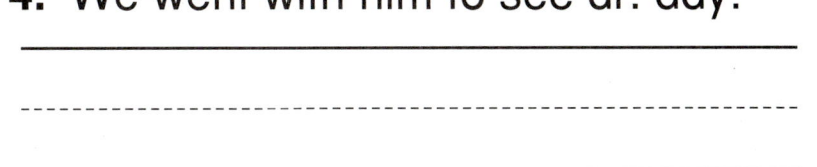

TRY THIS! Learning Log

Write the names of your best friends in your Learning Log. Remember to use capital letters.

Name _____

Best of Friends

A. Write the words where they belong in the puzzles.

bug   rug   mug   jug

B. Write words that rhyme with *bug* to complete the rhyme.

A bug on a _____ gave me a _____ .

28   SPELLING -ug   WARM FRIENDS Practice Book

Best of Friends

Name _____

Use the letters in the boxes to make rhyming words. Write the words to complete the rhymes.

b
G

All of **us**
_____
on the _____
_____
are friends of _____ .

r
s

We have **fun**
_____
when we play and _____
_____
out in the _____ .

gr
t

We see a **cub**
_____
looking for _____
_____
in a big tin _____ .

WARM FRIENDS Practice Book

SHORT VOWEL /u/u

29

Name _____

Read the letter. Write the word that best completes each sentence.

Dear Gregg,

I went for a walk with my _____ Fuzz.
day dog down

Fuzz saw a big bug _____ by. He ran.
buzz best sub

I had to _____ and puff to stay with him.
has here huff

What a walk! But it _____ fun.
want will was

Your friend,
Bif

Best of Friends

Name _____

Read the time on each clock. Write the word that best completes each sentence.

1. It is time to eat _____ .
   luck   let   lunch

2. Then I _____ with my friends.
   sad   chat   cap

3. It is time for my _____ .
   bad   bath   math

4. Now I can _____ TV.
   with   went   watch

What is your favorite time of day? Draw a clock in your Learning Log. Tell what you do at that time.

WARM FRIENDS Practice Book

DIGRAPHS /ch/ch, tch; /th/th   31

Name _____

The Shoe Town

Write the word that completes each sentence.

1. The three little pigs _____ a big tub.

    has   had   hello

2. They were going to _____ the mud.

    share   shell   so

3. They _____ to get in,

    but   big   began

    but it was too hot.

4. "Oh!" they said.

    "_____ get all red!"

    Was   When   We'll

32 VOCABULARY

WARM FRIENDS Practice Book

The Shoe Town

Name _____

5. A friend said, "_____ on."

    Her   Hang   Ham

6. "Don't _____ sad."

    but   by   be

7. "I _____ I know what to do."

  that   same   think

8. He began to _____ _____ on the mud.

  began   blow   blue

9. He made the pigs very _____.

  happy   here   have

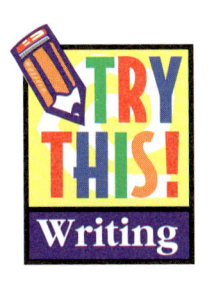

TRY THIS! Writing

How did the Big Bad Wolf get to be so friendly? Make up a story. Write it. Read it to a friend.

WARM FRIENDS Practice Book   VOCABULARY **33**

Name _____

The Shoe Town

Think about how the Shoe Town grew. What did the cow see at the beginning of the story? What did she see in the middle? What did she see at the end? Write it.

What the Cow Saw at the Beginning

What the Cow Saw in the Middle

What the Cow Saw at the End

34 SUMMARIZE AND RETELL

WARM FRIENDS Practice Book

If You Had a Mouse

Put a rope in her cage.
That will make her happy.

Get a bit of apple, too.
That will make her happy.

It will make you happy, too!

Harcourt Brace School Publishers

WARM FRIENDS Practice Book

CUT-OUT FOLD-UP BOOK 35

4

Put in a lot of paper.
That will make her happy.

2

Do you want a pet mouse? It will be up to you to make her happy.

Harcourt Brace School Publishers

5

Get seeds for her to eat.
That will make her happy.

7

Be a good friend to your mouse.
That will make her happy.

Directions: Help your child cut and fold the book.

36 CUT-OUT FOLD-UP BOOK

WARM FRIENDS Practice Book

The Shoe Town

Name _____

> The name of a **special place** begins with a capital letter.

Read the sentences. Circle the names of special places. Write each name correctly on the map.

I see rabbit hill.

I walk down happy road.

I go by sunny farm.

I stop to eat at yum yum house.

WARM FRIENDS Practice Book

GRAMMAR: Names of Special Places

Name _____

The Shoe Town

A. Say each word. Circle the words that rhyme with *big*.

big

1. dig	2. bug
3. girl	4. pig
5. wig	6. bun

B. Write words that rhyme with *big* to complete the poem.

I have a pink _____.

She put on a _____.

38   WORDS WITH -*ig*

WARM FRIENDS Practice Book

The Shoe Town

Name _____

Read each sentence and the two words under it. Use the two words to make a contraction and complete the sentence.

1. It's the cat!
   _____
   _____ run away.
   We   will

2. _____ come to catch us.
   He   will

3. But _____ not going to let him.
   I   am

4. _____ go over there.
   She   will

5. _____ get in here.
   I   will

WARM FRIENDS Practice Book

CONTRACTIONS: 'll, 'm   39

Name _____

The Shoe Town

A. Help the teacher line up these children in ABC order. Write 1, 2, 3, and 4 to show where they should be in each line.

A B C D E F G H I J K L M N O P Q R S T U V W X Y Z

Dan   Ann   Ben   Cath

Max   Nan   Peg   Liz

Jack   Fred   Sal   Tim

40 ALPHABETICAL ORDER

WARM FRIENDS Practice Book

Harcourt Brace School Publishers

The Shoe Town

Name _____

B. Circle the first letter in each word. Then write the words in ABC order. The words should describe each picture.

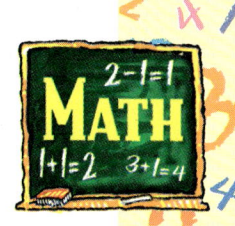

1. swimming   pig   one
   _____
   _____
   _____

2. hens   four   jumping
   _____
   _____
   _____

3. little   five   rabbits
   _____
   _____
   _____
   _____
   _____

How many animals are there in all? _____

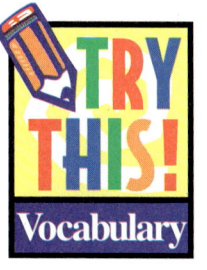

TRY THIS! Vocabulary

Write the ABCs in your Learning Log. Try to write an animal name that begins with each letter.

WARM FRIENDS Practice Book   ALPHABETICAL ORDER   41

Name _____

The Shoe Town

Complete the poem. Write the word that best completes each sentence and rhymes with the underlined word.

| duck   fun   mud   sun |

I love to <u>run</u>.
It is lots of _____.

I run and I <u>run</u>
out in the _____.

What bad <u>luck</u>!
I ran into a _____!

Did you hear that <u>thud</u>?
I fell in the _____.

SHORT VOWEL: /u/u

The Shoe Town

Name _____

Write the word that best completes the answer to each question.

1. What is a bee? A buzz with _____
   if   fizz   fuzz

2. What is this? An egg with _____
   logs   legs   is

3. What will he do? Huff and _____
   puff   ruff   off

4. What is this? A bug in a _____
   rag   rug   egg

5. What boys are with Dad? Dad's _____
   lots   let's   lads

WARM FRIENDS Practice Book

FINAL CONSONANTS: /z/s, zz; /f/f, ff; /g/g, gg

Name _____

Write the word that best completes each sentence.

1. Jan is not a _____ now.

   baby   bad   big

2. It is her _____.

   began   black   birthday

3. Friends came _____ here and there.

   for   from   or

4. Will we have fun _____ not?

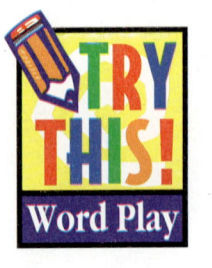

   old   or   off

Making Friends, Keeping Friends

TRY THIS! Word Play

How many words can you find in Happy Birthday? Write them in your Learning Log.

44 VOCABULARY   WARM FRIENDS   Practice Book

Making Friends, Keeping Friends

Name _____

5. The games _____.
   best   baby   begin

6. Friends get on the same _____.
   the   then   team

7. Mom yells the _____ "GO!"
   word   when   well

8. Then _____ one of us tugs!
   even   each   eat

9. We all _____ to win.
   team   try   trap

10. Then we all jump in the _____.
    water   word   when

WARM FRIENDS Practice Book

VOCABULARY 45

Name _____

Making Friends, Keeping Friends

**Circle the things that you learned in the story.
Write them inside the circle of friends.**

You can talk with a friend.
Friends have to talk all the time.
Sometimes friends play.
Friends do not get mad at all.
It is fun to be a friend.

46 SUMMARIZE AND RETELL

WARM FRIENDS Practice Book

Friends Always

1

Sometimes we can not be on the same team.
But we are always friends.

3

Sometimes one is up and one is down.
But we are always friends.

9

Good friends.
Dear friends.
Always friends.

8

Harcourt Brace School Publishers

WARM FRIENDS   Practice Book

CUT-OUT FOLD-UP BOOK   **47**

Sometimes we can not play the same games.
But we are always friends.

Sometimes we do not like the same things.
But we are always friends.

Sometimes we get sad or mad.
But we are always friends.

Sometimes we do not talk.
Not for a long time.
But we are always friends.

Directions: Help your child cut and fold the book.

48 CUT-OUT FOLD-UP BOOK

WARM FRIENDS Practice Book

Making Friends, Keeping Friends

Name _____

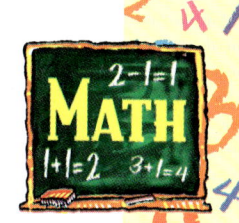

A naming word can name **one** person.
A naming word can name **more than one**.
Some naming words add **s** to name more than one.

Write the word that best completes each sentence.

1. One _____ is swimming.
   girl   girls

2. A _____ jumps in with her.
   friend   friends

3. Look! Here come two more _____.
   girl   girls

4. Now I can see three _____ swimming.
   friend   friends

WARM FRIENDS Practice Book

ONE AND MORE THAN ONE 49

Name _____

A. Say each word. Circle the words that rhyme with *fun*.

fun	
1. fan	2. bun
3. run	4. fish
5. game	6. sun

B. Write words that rhyme with *run* to complete the poem.

Let's run in the _____.

We will have _____.

50 WORDS WITH -*un* WARM FRIENDS Practice Book

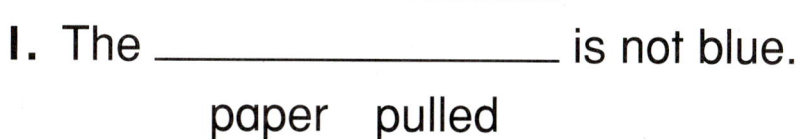

Name _____

Look at the pictures. Write the word that best completes each sentence.

1. The _____ is not blue.
   paper   pulled

2. Rick thinks _____ his dog.
   always   about

3. The duck is in the _____.
   walking   water

4. Beth likes _____.
   lemons   long

5. Liz _____ to paint.
   body   began

Name _____

Rex and Lilly Playtime

A. Write the word that completes each sentence.

1. Miss Rex said, "Hello, _____."
   class   cold   sad

2. "Are you _____ to begin?"
   read   ready   ride

3. "Let's _____ up now."
   with   want   warm

4. "Do you know _____?"
   hot   himself   how

Rex and Lilly Playtime

Name _____

5. "Look! I _____ do it."
   shell   saw   shall

6. Miss Rex began to jump and _____.
   same   swim   slide

7. Miss Rex loves to _____.
   dear   dance   down

B. Say the words in the box. Write each one where it belongs in the chart.

| class   dance   warm |

How to _____ up	How to _____	Things we do in _____
run	slide	reading
jump	step	math
put on a hat	dip	thinking

WARM FRIENDS Practice Book

VOCABULARY   53

Name _____

Rex and Lilly
Playtime

Think about the story and fill in the chart.

WHAT TIME IS IT?

WHAT DID REX THINK?
WHAT DID REX DO?

WHAT TIME IS IT?	WHAT DID REX THINK? / WHAT DID REX DO?
Time for dance class	
Time to warm up	
Time to dance	
Time to go home	

54 SUMMARIZE AND RETELL

WARM FRIENDS Practice Book

Harcourt Brace School Publishers

Animal Dances

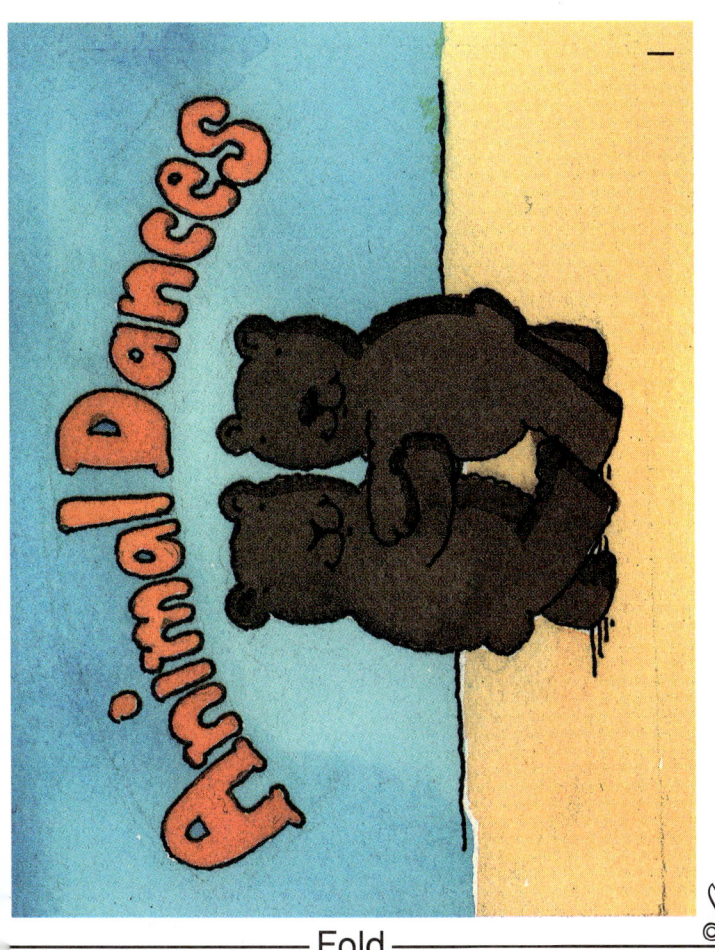

1

Bees can do a bee dance.

3

Seals can do a seal dance.

6

What dances can you do?

8

Harcourt Brace School Publishers

WARM FRIENDS Practice Book

CUT-OUT FOLD-UP BOOK 55

4

Birds can do a bird dance.

2

Animals can dance.
Do you know how?

— Fold —

— Fold —

Harcourt Brace School Publishers

A snake can do a snake dance.

Look! Even elephants can do an elephant dance.

5

7

Directions: Help your child cut and fold the book.

56   CUT-OUT FOLD-UP BOOK

WARM FRIENDS   Practice Book

Rex and Lilly Playtime

Name _____

Some naming words name the **days of the week.** The names of the days begin with capital letters.

Write the names of the days of the week to complete the sentences.

| Sunday | Monday | Tuesday | Wednesday |
| Thursday | Friday | Saturday |

1. It is _____ today.

2. The next day will be _____ .

3. I like _____ best of all.

4. I have fun on _____ and _____ .

Name _____

Rex and Lilly Playtime

A. Say each word. Circle the words that rhyme with *sack*.

sack

1. baby	2. pack
3. tack	4. ten
5. dog	6. track

B. Write another word that rhymes with *sack*. Then draw a picture of it.

58 WORDS WITH -*ack*

WARM FRIENDS Practice Book

Rex and Lilly Playtime

Name _____

Make this frog dance!

1. Put two long legs on it.
2. Put socks on it, too.
3. Make the frog and the legs green.
4. Make the socks red.

Name _____

Rex and Lilly Playtime

Look at these word parts. Put the beginnings and endings together to make words. Write the words under the pictures they match.

Beginnings   **Endings**

bas   sun   rab   cow   bit   boy   ket   set

1.

2.

3.

4.

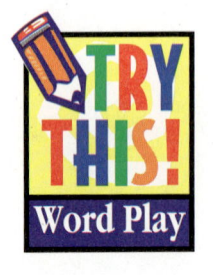

Choose two of the word parts. Make up a brand new word. Draw a picture to show what your word means.

TRY THIS! Word Play

60 WORD PARTS   WARM FRIENDS Practice Book

Rex and Lilly Playtime

Name _____

Read each sentence. Choose a contraction from the box for the underlined words. Then write the sentence again.

| You'll   I'm   She'll   I'll |

<u>I am</u> going to dance.
<u>I will</u> ask Rose.
<u>She will</u> dance with me.
<u>You will</u> see.

1. _____

2. _____

3. _____

4. _____

SKILLS AND STRATEGIES INDEX

How to make a Learning Log 1–2

DECODING
Cueing Systems
    Phonics in context **L3** 9
Phonics analysis
    Consonant correspondences
        Clusters, initial with *r* **L2** 11, 33
        Digraphs
            /ch/*ch, tch;* /th/*th* **L3** 19, 31
            /kw/*qu* **L2** 53
        Final
            /b/*b,* /n/*n,* **L1** 21, 33
            /t/*t,* /p/*p* **L1** 11, 33
            /k/*k, ck;* /l/*l, ll* **L2** 19, 45
            /ks/*x,* /m/*m,* /d/*d* **L2** 43, 56
            /f/*f, ff;* /g/*g;* /z/*s, zz* **L3** 30, 43
        Medial
            consonants /b/*b,* /g/*g,* /m/*m,* /t/*t* **L3** 51
            double consonants **L2** 31
    Vowel correspondences
        /a/*a* **L1** 12-13, 23, 34
        /e/*e* **L2** 9-10, 23
        /i/*i* **L2** 41-42, 57, 67
        /o/*o* **L1** 31, 57, 68
        /u/*u* **L3** 29, 42
        letter pattern CVC **L1** 65
Structural analysis
    Contractions
        'll, 'm **L3** 39, 61
        'm, 's (is) **L1** 32
        n't, 's **L2** 32, 44, 68
    Inflections
        -ed, -ing **L1** 43; **L2** 20
        -s **L1** 22, 35
        -s, -ed, -ing **L1** 56, 66
    Word parts **L2** 65; **L3** 60

VOCABULARY
Context clues and pictures **L2** 21-22
Key Words **L1** 4-5, 14-15, 24-25, 36-37, 46-47, 58-59; **L2** 2-3, 12-13, 24-25, 34-35, 46-47, 58-59; **L3** 2-3, 12-13, 22-23, 32-33, 44-45, 52-53
Rhyming words **L1** 53, 67

COMPREHENSION
Classifying **L1** 54-55
Drawing conclusions **L3** 20-21
Reality and fantasy **L1** 44-45
Sequence **L2** 54-55; **L3** 10-11
Summarize and retell **L1** 6, 16, 26, 38, 48, 60; **L2** 4, 14, 26, 36, 48, 60; **L3** 4, 14, 24, 34, 46, 54

LITERARY APPRECIATION
Story elements **L2** 66

STUDY SKILLS
Alphabetical order **L3** 40-41
Following directions **L3** 59

GRAMMAR
Days of the week **L3** 57
I; End marks **L2** 63
Naming words
    one and more than one **L3** 49
    places, animals, and things **L3** 17
    people **L3** 7
    special places **L3** 37
    special names and titles of people **L3** 27
Sentences **L1** 19, 29
    asking **L1** 63
    definition **L2** 51
    parts
        joining naming **L2** 17
        joining telling **L2** 39
        naming **L2** 7
        telling **L2** 29
    telling **L1** 51
    word order **L1** 41
    write one's name **L1** 9

SPELLING
Words with
    Initial Consonants **L1** 10

-ack **L3** 58	-en **L2** 30	-ip **L2** 52
-ad **L2** 64	-et **L2** 8	-op **L1** 64
-an **L1** 42	-ick **L2** 40	-ot **L1** 30
-ap **L1** 20	-ig **L3** 38	-ug **L3** 28
-at **L1** 52	-ill **L3** 18	-un **L3** 50
-ell **L2** 18	-in **L3** 8	